Sharper Than a Two-Edged Sword

Sharper Than a Two-Edged Sword

PREACHING, TEACHING, AND LIVING THE BIBLE

Edited by

Michael Root & James J. Buckley

WILLIAM B. EERDMANS PUBLISHING COMPANY
GRAND RAPIDS, MICHIGAN / CAMBRIDGE, U.K.

© 2008 Wm. B. Eerdmans Publishing Co.

Published 2008 by
Wm. B. Eerdmans Publishing Co.
2140 Oak Industrial Drive N.E., Grand Rapids, Michigan 49505 /
P.O. Box 163, Cambridge CB3 9PU U.K.

Printed in the United States of America

14 13 12 11 10 09 08   7 6 5 4 3 2 1

Library of Congress Cataloging-in-Publication Data

Sharper than a two-edged sword: preaching, teaching, and living the Bible /
    edited by Michael Root & James J. Buckley.
        p.   cm.
    Includes bibliographical references and index.
    ISBN 978-0-8028-6271-6 (pbk.: alk. paper)
    1. Bible — Criticism, interpretation, etc. — Congresses.
    2. Bible — Homiletical use — Congresses.
    3. Bible — Study and teaching — Congresses.
    4. Christian life — Biblical teaching — Congresses.
    I. Root, Michael, 1940-   II. Buckley, James Joseph, 1947-

    BS511.3.S53   2008
    220.6 — dc22

                                                    2008012450

www.eerdmans.com

Contents

INTRODUCTION

The Biblical Sword in the Cause of Peace

The psalmist declares that "Your word is a lamp to my feet and a light on my path." Today an increasing number of people of faith are less certain about the light offered in Scripture. They are not sure how to live the life of faith. In turn, many clergy and laity find themselves uncertain how to preach and teach the Bible today. In May 2006 the Center for Catholic and Evangelical Theology and the Duke Divinity School sponsored a conference for clergy and laity to discuss how to read the Bible theologically in these circumstances — how to preach and teach it in the parish in our contemporary context, and live the sacred story in faith. The essays here are collected from that conference.

The title of this volume is a claim that these essays, in and with their differences, share at least three characteristics. First, the word of God (not necessarily the preaching and teaching of men and women) is "sharper than any two-edged sword" (Heb. 4:12). The words of men and women in preaching and teaching and living the Bible are responses to this word of God — and are sharp, with the right edges for peacemaking, only as such responses. In this sense reading Scripture with the eyes of faith is reading Scripture in response to God's reading of the story of all creation and Israel, of Jesus Christ and the Spirit's communion of saints. This basic conviction shapes all these essays, whether the essays are by preachers or exegetes or theologians.

Second, preaching, teaching, and living the Bible are firmly yet delicately intertwined in the communion of saints. Some may be tempted to restrict preaching to pastors, teaching to academics, and living the Bible to the rest of God's people. But this would be a worldly division of labor, far from the peaceable church. Pastors and teachers know the challenge of practicing what they preach and teach. And those who are not official preachers and teachers still seek to live the word of God. They know that the Bible they have heard preached and taught is an internal rather than external ingredient of the faith they live. Parents as well as pastors and priests preach and teach by what they say as well as by what they do — each and all, again, in response to God's word. Such an intertwining of preaching, teaching, and living the Bible in the communion of saints is another common presumption of these essays.

Third, there are distinctive ministries of preaching and teaching in the church, as well as other liturgical and diaconal ministries. This holy diversity also means that there are disputes not only between those who do and who do not read Scripture with the eyes of faith but also among those who do thus read Scripture. Some preachers may doubt the relevance to their practice of much of what goes on in the academy, just as some teachers wonder if some preachers have studied the text on which they are preaching. Some of those seeking to live the Bible may wonder what these disputes between preachers and teachers have to do with their lives. Readers will hear some of these disputes in the background and sometimes the foreground of these essays. But this will happen in unusual ways. Theologians lament the way they have unfortunately reflected on Scripture more than they have actually used it. Exegetes not only explicate the text but actually use Scripture to shape lives. Pastors here face the challenge of not simply preaching the Word but reflecting on that practice. The disputes do not go away. But they are embedded in a communion larger than themselves, all in response to God's (s)word. The biblical sword is thus in the service of peace.

Because the essays exhibit this intertwining, we have found it impossible to order them by theme. We have therefore placed the essays in the order in which they were given at the conference: a theologian reflecting on exegesis at the beginning (Reno) and an exegete reflecting on theological exegesis at the end (Hays), with essays in the middle in which a preacher not only preaches but reflects on preaching (Breidenthal), theologians not only teach about Scripture but use Scripture to form minds and hearts and lives (Jenson, Pauw), and a biblical exegete not simply explicates texts but brings them to bear on our lives (Davis). Preachers may wish to begin with the essay of the preacher on preaching, biblical scholars with the exercises of the exegetes on theological exegesis, theologians with the work of theologians who actually use Scripture. It matters less where readers begin than that readers seek the conversations and connections among the essays. We invite readers thus to seek the common themes as well as the differences between the essays as they use the essays in their own concrete circumstances — and thus to replicate and expand the incomplete conversation we had at the conference.

MICHAEL ROOT
Lutheran Theological
Southern Seminary

JAMES J. BUCKLEY
Loyola College in Maryland

Theology and Biblical Interpretation

R. R. Reno

When the core group that would become the Scripture Project gathered for the first time, Ellen Davis reports they came to a consensus. "The most fundamental need," the group quickly agreed, is "to learn again to read and teach the Bible confessionally within mainstream North American and European Christianity."[1] It is a judgment that I think is widespread. Theology, understood as the knowledge of and skill in analyzing, defending, and applying the doctrines of the church, is not in adequate contact with modern knowledge of and skill in interpreting the Bible.[2] This bifurcation affects all aspects of Christian experience. The way in which we read and

1. "Teaching the Bible Confessionally in the Church," in *The Art of Reading Scripture,* ed. Ellen F. Davis and Richard B. Hays (Grand Rapids: Eerdmans, 2003), p. 9.

2. See Walter Moberly, *The Bible, Theology, and Faith: A Study in Abraham and Jesus* (Cambridge: Cambridge University Press, 2000). According to Moberly, modern biblical study has created a "curious situation." "To be Christian means, at least in part," he continues, "the acceptance and appropriation of certain theological doctrines and patterns of living. Yet the task of reading the Bible 'critically' has regularly been defined precisely in terms of the exclusion of these doctrines and patterns of living from the interpretive process" (p. 5). The confessionally committed are not the only people to notice this disjunction. Many modern biblical scholars bemoan the persistent Christian disregard for advanced results of biblical scholarship. Thus, Van Harvey observes, "Anyone teaching the origins of Christianity to college undergraduates or divinity students cannot help but be struck by the enormous gap between what the average layperson believes to be historically true about Jesus of Nazareth and what a great majority of New Testament scholars have concluded" (from "New Testament Scholarship and Christian Belief," in *Jesus in History and Myth,* ed. R. Joseph Hoffman and Gerald A. Larue [Buffalo: Prometheus, 1986], p. 193).

teach the Bible is removed from and does not inform the way in which we talk about our faith and organize our lives. It is hard to imagine a more fundamental crisis.[3]

"Theological exegesis" seems to describe the mode of reading that we hope can overcome the alienation of theology from biblical study. The series I am editing, the *Brazos Theological Commentary on the Bible,* certainly uses the term in this sense. But I must confess that I find the concept of theological exegesis opaque and even problematic. Too often we think of theological interpretation as something distinct from textually grounded analysis. For example, in the general introduction to the *Interpretation* series the editors tell us that exegesis involves a double task involving seemingly two different mental operations: "to deal with what the texts say and to discern their meaning for faith and life." Krister Stendahl's old distinction between "what it meant for them" and "what it means for us" continues to echo.

The problem is that the church has acknowledged no such distinction, or at least never allowed the distinction to move to the center of the exegetical project. Christian readers recognized that certain texts required grammatical clarification. They saw that in some instances exposition demanded observations about historical context. At times, doctrine is explicitly brought to bear. At other times, moral conclusions are drawn and contemporary applications are made. Yet all this diversity of focus and

---

3. One of the most important twentieth-century Protestant theological moves has been to interpret this crisis as a positive development. By this account, the genius of the Reformation was the shattering of all works of the law by the doctrine of justification. The modern application of historical-critical principles to doctrine and Scripture completes the Reformers' project. Critical historical method undermines these forms of authority, and this clears the way for a true and pure Protestant atmosphere of faith entirely free from temptation to rest in external forms of assurance, including the literal sense of the Bible itself. For a classic statement of this argument, see Gerhard Ebeling, "The Significance of the Critical Historical Method for Church and Theology in Protestantism," first published in 1950 and reprinted in revised form in *Word and Faith* (London: SCM, 1963), pp. 17-61. For a broader statement of the same argument, see Paul Tillich's characterizations of the Protestant Principle in *The Protestant Era* (Chicago: University of Chicago Press, 1948). For an illustration of consequent mentality, see John Shelby Spong, *Rescuing the Bible from Fundamentalism* (San Francisco: HarperSanFrancisco, 1992).

concern functioned within a single interpretive enterprise. Pre-critical readers did not seek a "theological meaning" as something over and against another "historical meaning." They distinguished between good and bad exegesis, not between theological exegesis and some other possible and equally legitimate mode of interpretation.

With the sobering witness of the tradition in mind, I want to take a stab at describing the mode of interpretation we all seem to want, and I want to do so without relying upon methodological or hermeneutical contrasts between theological and historical-critical methods. I want to give an account of biblical exegesis that does not suggest that reading the Bible ("deal with what the text says") is somehow different from thinking about God's gracious love. I will try to do so in three ways. First, as befits a systematic theologian, I want to describe the relationship between doctrine (by which I mean not only official teachings but also the larger public form of the church, which includes liturgical practice, moral formation, and spiritual discipline) and Scripture. It is a linkage that we must seek if we are to be both consistent and alive in our beliefs. Second, I plan to give an example of my own effort to read "theologically." Finally, I will conclude by offering some programmatic remarks that return to the question of modern historical-critical study and its relation to theological interpretation.

I

In the aftermath of the Reformation, the interpretation of the Bible became a point of contest, and the relationship between doctrine and Scripture was variously defined. But in every case a profound conformity of doctrine with Scripture was asserted. For most of the post-Reformation period, the Catholic Church insisted upon an almost complete correspondence, allowing only for the possibility that biblical exegesis, like doctrine, can develop toward fuller and fuller exposition of already recognized truths.[4] The Protestant tradition's interest in ongoing reform of the church

---

4. This was in some measure modified at Vatican II. See *Dei Verbum,* ¶22.

made the relationship between doctrine and Scripture less static, but the underlying logic was similar. What the Bible says and what the church teaches may not be in full accord at present, but they should be, and the goal of both exegesis and theology is to maximize this correspondence.

The principle of apostolic legitimacy motivates this close correspondence between doctrine and Scripture. The logic is transparent. If the Bible teaches x and the church teaches not x, then either the Bible teaches the truth or the church teaches the truth. But since the true church of Christ teaches the gospel, and since the Bible is the sacred and canonical witness to the gospel, such a disjunction is intolerable.

I think it is worthwhile to see this logic in action in confessional documents. For the presumption of apostolic legitimacy helps explain why "theological exegesis," that is to say exegesis in accordance with church teaching, must be the best, most compelling reading.

At the Council of Trent we find juxtaposition between scriptural interpretation based upon "personal judgment" and reading guided by "holy mother church." It is intolerable, Trent teaches, that private persons should set about to produce interpretations contrary to those established by the traditions of the church. To prevent the possibility of any disjunction between biblical interpretation and church teaching, the Council of Trent provides a crucial post-Reformation definition of magisterial authority. It is the function of the church, we read, "to judge the true sense and interpretation of the sacred scriptures."[5]

The First and Second Vatican Councils reiterate this affirmation of magisterial authority. As we read in Vatican I's *Dogmatic Constitution on the Catholic Faith (De Fide):*

> Now since the decree on the interpretation of holy scripture, profitably made by the council of Trent, with the intention of constraining rash speculation, has been wrongly interpreted by some, we renew that decree and declare its meaning to be as follows: that in matters of faith and morals, belonging as they do to the establishing of Christian doctrine, that the meaning of holy scripture must be held to be the true

5. Session 4, second decree.

4

one, which holy mother church held and holds, since it is her right to judge the true meaning and interpretation of holy scripture.[6]

The Second Vatican Council's *Dogmatic Constitution on Divine Revelation (Dei Verbum)* provides a much more extensive, plastic, and complex account of the role and interpretation of Scripture in the life of the church.[7] But the underlying logic remains intact. As we read, "The task of authentically interpreting the word of God . . . has been entrusted only to those charged with the church's ongoing teaching function, whose authority is exercised in the name of Jesus Christ."[8]

For all the differences between Protestant and Catholic, on the principle of apostolic legitimacy the two traditions are as one. The Lutheran Formula of Concord opens with the Protestant principle of *sola scriptura.* "We believe, confess, and teach," the Formula states, "that the only rule and norm according to which all dogmas and all doctors ought to be assessed and judged, is no other thing than the prophetic and apostolic writings of both the Old and of the New Testament."[9] In the Reformed tradition, the Westminster Confession provides a more detailed discussion of the necessity of the illumination of the Holy Spirit in right reading, as well as the proper scope for natural reason in practical considerations of church order, but the basic principle remains the same. "The Supreme Judge, by which all controversies of religion are to be determined, and all decrees of councils, opinions of ancient writers, doctrines of men, and private spirits,

---

6. *De Fide,* chapter 2. The restatement and clarification of Trent was motivated by concern about two nineteenth-century opinions, both of which sought to loosen the bond between church teaching and scriptural interpretation. One argued that Trent's decree was purely disciplinary and not dogmatic in consequence. The second argued that Trent required assent to dogmas officially derived from Scripture, but not assent to the particular interpretations. For background, see Jean-Michel-Alfred Vacant, *Études théologiques sur les constitutions du Concile de Vatican,* Tome 1 (Paris: Delhomme et Briguet, 1895), pp. 520-21.

7. In an important contrast to the seemingly one-sided ascription of authority to the *magisterium* in earlier statements, Vatican II states, "This teaching function is not above the word of God but stands at its service, teaching nothing but what is handed down, accordingly as it devotedly listens, reverently preserves and faithfully transmits the word of God, by divine command and with the help of the Holy Spirit" (*Dei Verbum,* ¶10).

8. *Dei Verbum,* ¶10.

9. Epitome, Of the Compendious Rule and Norm, I.

are to be examined, and in whose sentence we are to rest, can be no other than the Holy Spirit speaking in the Scripture."[10]

This is not a paper in ecumenical theology, so I cannot address the real differences between Catholic and Lutheran and Reformed views on the link between doctrine and biblical interpretation. There are clear disagreements about the role of the church in establishing and sustaining this relationship, with the Catholic side thinking a *magisterium* indispensable and the Protestant side tending to think it fatal. However, I hope that it is clear how closely these confessional traditions agree. And how could it be otherwise? For the principle of apostolic legitimacy requires the following conclusion. What is taught by the church must be substantially in accord with what the Bible says, or to put the issue in a more cautious double negative, the church cannot teach that which is substantially discordant with what the Bible says. Even aggressively non-confessional Protestants adopt this assumption. They reject the instrumentalities of written confessions precisely because they think such human-made documents stand in the way of the complete correspondence between church teaching and biblical preaching. The two should be one and the same ecclesial act, not two different aspects of church life that need to be brought into accordance. So, however bitter are debates about church authority, confessional documents, theories of inerrancy, or methods of interpretation, the principle of apostolic legitimacy is not itself controversial. It is instead the great point of agreement around which ecumenical controversies swirl.

With this close relationship between church doctrine and the content of the Bible in mind, I think we can make an initial approach to providing a more precise definition of theological interpretation. The problem is not that something labeled "theology" has not adequately engaged something else called "biblical studies." We do not want for interdisciplinary study. Instead, we are facing a collective crisis. We are told that the doctrine of the Trinity is the great, foundational ecumenical doctrine of Christianity — and we are told that it is not to be found in the Bible. We are told that Jesus Christ is the Messiah who fulfills the law and the prophets — and we are told that such a reading of the Old Testament is an abuse of the text. I could go on

10. Chapter 1.

with more examples, but we all know the phenomenon. What the churches teach and what biblical scholars tell us is in the Bible seem at odds. I submit, therefore, that theological exegesis is, at minimum, any reading that moves in the opposite direction. An interpretation is theological insofar as it shows the ways in which church teaching accords with what the Bible says.

At this point I can imagine a certain discomfort. Is the purpose of exegesis to prove doctrine, as if doctrine were the great vehicle of divine truth and not the scriptures themselves? I think the discomfort is justified, for in both Protestant and Catholic traditions there has been a tendency to see doctrine as the purified, reasoned, and reconciled "content" of Scripture.[11] If we would but learn our Baltimore Catechism, then we would be fully formed in God's truth. But this cannot be true, for it is precisely a doctrine of the church that, while doctrines may teach truths about God, they do not reveal God. As the First Vatican Council observes, revelation is contained in Scripture and what is called the "unwritten traditions," both of which "were received by the apostles from the lips of Christ himself." God's living Word is to be found in this apostolic memory, and not in the subsequent doctrinal tradition. One could not claim to participate in the saving truth of Christ if one memorizes all of Denzinger but does not attend mass or fails to read the Bible.

Here we see the other side of theological exegesis. The principle of apostolic legitimacy drives exegesis toward a way of reading that links doc-

---

11. See, for example, a late nineteenth-century dogmatic handbook, *A Manual of Catholic Theology*, ed. Joseph Wilhelm and Thomas Scannell (London: Kegan Paul, Trench, Trübner, 1890). Doctrine is described as "materially complete," "formally perfect," and capable of universal application. In contrast, Scripture lacks "systematic arrangement," is "often obscure," and is "exposed to many false interpretations." Furthermore, the historical nature of Scripture means that its great truths are "expressed in the metaphorical language of the East." As a result, Scripture is largely "unfit for the general use of people" (p. 59). This elevation of doctrine over Scripture dominates the encyclical *Humani Generis* (1950), and theology is assigned the task of drawing out the implications of church doctrine, and showing how Scripture supports doctrine (see ¶21).

There is nothing uniquely Roman about this supersession of Scripture by doctrine. See Friedrich Schleiermacher's reasoning in *The Christian Faith*, ¶27. The conclusion is arresting: "The confessional documents of the Evangelical Church, collectively, are, as it were, given prior place to the New Testament Scriptures themselves" (27.1).

trine to Scripture, but the link is not probative, or not merely probative. Theological exegesis also serves the principle of apostolic vitality. Under the influence of the sustained criticisms of doctrinalized and deracinated modes of Christian formation, the Second Vatican Council gave urgent and eloquent voice to the need for a re-scripturalized faith. It is not the case that the church draws truths out of Scripture, encodes them into doctrines, and then moves on.[12] As the Council teaches, the church never ceases to receive "the bread of life from the one table of God's word and Christ's body," and "accordingly all the church's preaching, no less than the whole Christian religion, ought to be nourished and ruled by holy scripture."[13] No matter how correct doctrine might be in some formal sense, the project of bringing the biblical word to bear upon the life of the church is an ongoing, perpetual task. "There is such force and power in the word of God," teaches the Council, "that it stands as the church's support and strength, affording her children sturdiness in faith, food for the soul and a pure and unfailing fount of spiritual life."[14] The apostolic legitimacy of church teaching must be infused by the apostolic vitality of Scripture.

On the imperative of apostolic vitality the Protestant tradition has always insisted, and therefore, I think we can enlarge our definition of theological exegesis without controversy.[15] Not only does a properly theological interpretation seek to show the conformity of church teaching with

---

12. As Joseph Ratzinger observes in his commentary on *Dei Verbum*, the history of discussion at the Council suggests that "there was a gradual reduction of the idea of progress," and he registers his own view that "from an ecumenical point of view, the only sensible thing is to give up the idea of progress." The primary dynamic is one of return and renewal. Doctrine does not advance beyond Scripture; instead, doctrine brings the church back to Scripture (*Commentary on the Documents of Vatican II*, vol. 3, ed. Herbert Vorgrimler [New York: Herder & Herder, 1969], p. 266).

13. *Dei Verbum*, ¶21.

14. *Dei Verbum*, ¶21.

15. In the shadow of centuries of Protestant and Catholic polemics, we tend to turn questions of vitality back to legitimacy. If we are Protestant, we tend to think of the living Word of Scripture as a challenge to the authority of doctrine. If we are Catholic, we tend to think of any challenge to doctrine as an impermissible challenge to the legitimacy of the church. In some cases, questions of legitimacy are rightly placed front and center, but it is also important to see the way in which Scripture judges our teaching superficial and lifeless rather than erroneous or invalid.

what the Bible says, theological exegesis also reads Scripture as the living language of faith. Or perhaps more accurately, precisely insofar as it shows the conformity of Scripture and teaching, theological exegesis saturates the life of the church with what the Bible says. To put the matter in a formula, the more readily a reading of the Bible enters into the life and practice of the church, the more fully theological is the interpretation.

With this brief outline of the principle of apostolic legitimacy and imperative of apostolic vitality, I have defined theological exegesis without recourse to contrasts between historical-critical and other modes of reading. Interpretation should draw upon whatever intellectual methods seem appropriate. It is a conceit of modernity that method is foundational, a conceit long shown false by the actual practice of modern science. What matters are the ends sought. We want commerce between scientific theory and data that allows us to enter more fully into the world as it is. In the same way, we seek exegesis that links doctrine with Scripture in such a way that we can better inhabit the gospel. Therefore, interpretation is theological insofar as it shows the concord of doctrine with Scripture and maximizes the penetration of Scripture into the life and teaching of the church.

We are so accustomed to thinking in terms of methods and techniques rather than ends and goals that my definition of theological exegesis may seem an illusion of logic rather than a real possibility for Christian readers of the Bible. The old Stendhal distinction between what it meant and what it means, between reading the text "responsibly" and reading it "piously," has a powerful grip on us. We worry that without a distinct and prior role for critical historical reading, our exegesis will lack credibility and discipline. For these reasons, I want to flesh out just how these ends might shape exegetical practice, and I will do so by offering an instance of my own adventure in scriptural interpretation.

II

Consider the first verses of Genesis. Here we find biblical material both ambiguous and fraught. The Hebrew admits of different senses. Should we read the first verse as "In the beginning God created," conveying the sense that we are at the absolute beginning? Or should we read this opening verse as "In the beginning, when God created," now suggesting the more modest idea that we are being told about the first stage in a process that might be otherwise part of a larger whole? And furthermore, what are we to make about the next verse and its mention of the unformed earth and the darkness and the face of the waters? Did God make the heavens and earth out of a pre-existing primal substance? Does the divine beginning operate over and against a counter-beginning, an unformed earth, a darkness and chaos that somehow pre-exists the beginning?

In his *Unfinished Literal Commentary on Genesis,* Augustine raises these questions and offers a variety of interpretive suggestions. Augustine notes that the Bible does not provide every detail, so we can justly suppose that in the first moment God creates all the elements, the formless earth and the darkness and the water, and this can be conceived of in many different ways. But it is clear that loyalty to church doctrine is guiding Augustine on this point. As he says, "Whichever of these opinions is true, we must believe that God is the Maker and Creator of all things."[16] To recall our definition of theological exegesis, Augustine reads so as to affirm the principle of apostolic legitimacy. *Creatio ex nihilo,* creation out of nothing, is normative doctrine, and Augustine brings his reading into conformity with church teaching.

As modern men and women we are likely to step back and say, "Yes, of course, Augustine accepted the authority of doctrine, and look what happens. He is indifferent to what the Bible really says." The plain sense of the first verses suggests that there was *something* upon which God acted in creation. Furthermore, adopting the historicist mode of analysis, we can adduce the many combat myths from ancient literature, and we can show how the Old Testament often pictures the origins of the world in the same fashion. Aside from 2 Maccabees 7:28, the many declarations of God's creative sovereignty and power throughout the Bible do not specify creation out of nothing.[17] It would seem, then, the doctrine of *creatio ex nihilo* pre-

16. *Unfinished Literal Interpretation of Genesis,* 4.

17. For a contemporary rejection of *creatio ex nihilo* that highlights the lack of support in the Old Testament and advances a theological critique of the doctrine, see Jon D. Levenson, *Creation and the Persistence of Evil* (San Francisco: Harper & Row, 1988).

sents a classic case of preconceived theological ⸱
rigid system of doctrine is being imposed upon Sci⸱⸱
own voice. "It is one thing to accept responsibility for s⸱⸱
dance of Scripture and doctrine," we say, "but we must be ⸱
the text in the process."

The reaction is common, and one of the great dogmas of ⸱⸱
biblical study has been to exclude doctrine from exegesis. As Benja⸱⸱ ⸱n
Jowett wrote more than one hundred years ago, the role of the interpreter
is to recover "the simple words" of Scripture. This requires the reader to
"clear away the remains of dogmas, systems, controversies," which our ecclesiastical imaginations have perversely imposed upon the text. By returning to the text in its purity, Jowett promises, we will commune with
the minds of the original authors, and scriptures once smothered by doctrine will return to life.[18]

Unfortunately, the effect has been otherwise. Insofar as actual
churches continue to recite the Nicene Creed, any reading of Genesis 1
that fails to conclude that the text does not contradict the doctrine of
creatio ex nihilo effectively removes these verses from the functional piety
of believers, generally weakening the role of the Bible in the life of the
church. How can one affirm the doctrine that God creates out of nothing,
a doctrine embedded in the creeds and liturgy, and agree that the Bible
teaches otherwise, without relaxing the relationship between doctrine,
worship, and Scripture? This is not an isolated instance. It occurs whenever a biblical interpreter concludes that the Bible says something other
than the church teaches. Instead of coming to life, the voice of Scripture is
muffled, even silenced.

Must we then choose between loyalty to doctrine and attentiveness
to the textual reality of Scripture? Must we engage in exegetical finger-
crossing in order to keep the Bible as the Scripture of the church? To say
"yes" involves a massive misunderstanding of the nature and role of doctrine in scriptural interpretation. Classical doctrine is not *sui generis*. Doctrines such as *creatio ex nihilo* guide an overall reading of Scripture that

18. See "On the Interpretation of Scripture," in *Essays and Reviews* (London: Parker,
1860), pp. 338-39.

claims to be the most satisfactory, and because most satisfactory, most capable of bringing Scripture to life. Furthermore, there is nothing complacent about accepting the authority of doctrine in the work of exegesis. It is precisely the *difficulty* of bringing Scripture and doctrine into some kind of intellectually and spiritually satisfactory relationship that infuses exegesis with urgency, energy, and creativity. This difficulty may tempt us to escape by way of conventional dogmatic solutions or superficial exegesis. The Christian tradition provides us with many examples. But at least we will be protected from the anodyne and vague theological gestures that characterize so much modern biblical interpretation.[19]

In order to illustrate how doctrine is scriptural in substance and energizing in effect, I need to show how *creatio ex nihilo* arises from a complex array of exegetical judgments that operate across the entire biblical text. This set of interpretive judgments maximizes the plain sense of the scriptures, supports a metaphysical framework for coherent affirmations of that plain sense, and encourages a christological focus for biblical interpretation as a whole. For these reasons, allowing the doctrine of creation out of nothing to guide a reading of Genesis 1 amounts to a decision to allow the larger witness of Scripture to guide interpretation.

In the first place, the Old Testament campaign against idolatry has a recurring structure. Idols are not weak, ineffective, or inadequate; they are empty and lifeless. Those who set themselves up against the LORD's commands "are nothing; their molten images are empty wind" (Isa. 41:29). "The makers of idols go into confusion" (Isa. 45:16). For idols are not evil powers, nor can they represent a primal potency or reality upon which God might have operated in creation. Instead, idols are "like scarecrows," and "they cannot do evil, neither is it in them to do good" (Jer. 10:5).

The New Testament carries forward the same view of idols. They are lifeless and powerless. Paul consistently explains the futility of idols by appeal to God's creative uniqueness (see Acts 14:15; 17:24). For this reason, Paul is indifferent to any thought that meat sacrificed to idols might be in-

---

19. For a survey of examples, see my essay, "Biblical Theology and Theological Exegesis," in *Out of Egypt: Biblical Theology and Biblical Interpretation,* ed. Craig Bartholomew, Mary Healy, Karl Moeller, and Robin Parry (London: Paternoster, 2004), pp. 385-408.

fected by a hidden, shameful potency (see 1 Cor. 8). Idols are not malign; they are empty and vacant. The danger is not that idols will bewitch by some internal, semi-divine power. They transfix because we fill the vacancy of idols with the noisy gongs and clanging symbols of empty prophecy and pseudo-mystery (1 Cor. 13:1).

Throughout Scripture, claims about lifeless idols and their dangerous nullity are made against the background of larger affirmations of God's creative sovereignty. In each instance, we find an implicit ontological parsimony. Because God creates out of nothing, there is nothing *(nihil)* other than the one true God and the set of all things he has made. Thus, idolatry is not a simple mistake or miscalculation. It is not a loyalty to a semi-divine or primeval power that cannot measure up to the power and glory of the LORD. Idolatry is loyalty to *nihil*, a devotion to lifelessness, and for this reason, the Old Testament often portrays idolatry as the paradigm of sin. Idolatry encourages and reflects a desire for nothingness, a choice of death. St. Paul's account of sin begins with a primordial turn from the living God whose creative glory is readily "perceived in the things that have been made" (Rom. 1:20) toward "images" (Rom. 1:20-23). The baleful genealogy simply reiterates the judgments of the Old Testament. There is no place to stand between God and creation — and to try to do so only results in a crazy, self-defeating loyalty to nothingness. Not surprisingly, therefore, the themes of idolatry and loyalty set the stage for the explicit affirmation of *creatio ex nihilo* in 2 Maccabees 7:28.[20]

The second reason for submitting our reading of Genesis 1 to the control of the doctrine of *creatio ex nihilo* concerns the apparent conflict between two biblical claims about God. On the one hand, we read, "Behold, the heaven and the heaven of the heavens cannot contain thee" (1 Kings 8:27). God is wholly other and cannot be framed within the finite

---

20. For a patristic analysis of idolatry that presumes *creatio ex nihilo*, see St. Athanasius, *Contra Gentes* 8 (NPNF II, vol. 4, p. 8). For a contemporary study of idolatry that emphasizes the importance of the ontological parsimony (though cast in modern, phenomenological terms), see Jean-Luc Marion, *The Idol and Distance*, trans. Thomas A. Carlson (New York: Fordham University Press, 2001). For my own analysis of the perversely inflating role of the vacuum of nothingness in idolatry, see "Pride and Idolatry," *Interpretation* 60, no. 2 (April 2006): 166-80.

world. On the other hand, God is a character within the biblical story. He commands and speaks, and, in places such as Genesis 17:1, "appears." In the New Testament, classical doctrine teaches that God is present as the incarnate second person of the Trinity. So, which shall it be? Is God without or within? Is God wholly other or part of the unfolding drama of finite creation? These questions concern more than intra-scriptural tension. They also have to do with contemporary intuitions about the universality of truth and the particularity of cultures. The bumper sticker declaration, "My God is too big for any one religion," reflects the conviction that one must by loyal to 1 Kings 8:27 to the exclusion of Genesis 17:1. One must affirm the universal deity in contradiction to the LORD who elects a particular nation. The contrastive choice between universality and particularity is all the more dramatic in classical christology. Divine transcendence would seem utterly inconsistent with incarnation.

The ontological parsimony of *creatio ex nihilo* helps us resolve the apparent contradiction between the transcendence and presence of God. The doctrine of creation out of nothing teaches that God is in relation to absolutely nothing other than himself prior to creation, because there is nothing prior to creation for God not to be. As Exodus 3:14 teaches, God is who he is simply because he is who he is, and not because he is not something else.

Because *creatio ex nihilo* formulates God's transcendence in terms of uniqueness rather than as a supremacy or priority over some sort of primal matter, the transcendence of God is consistent with his immediacy and presence to finite reality. God leaves nothing behind; he betrays or contradicts nothing "divine" by drawing near. For there is no divine "stuff" other than the singular "I am." Thus, a biblical reader need not choose between the universal God and the LORD who acts in space and time.[21] Nor need the reader parse divinity and humanity in the unified person of Jesus Christ.[22] In contrast, a reading of Genesis 1:2 that contra-

---

21. On this point and with the same argument, see St. Thomas, *Summa Theologica*, I.13.7.resp.

22. See Origen, *Contra Celsum* 4.5. For a helpful discussion of the way in which *creatio ex nihilo* provides crucial background for christological doctrine, see Robert Sokolowski, *The God of Faith & Reason: Foundations of Christian Theology* (Washington, DC: Catholic University Press, 1982), pp. 31-40.

dicts *creatio ex nihilo* and its implied ontological parsimony will under-mine the capacity of scriptural readers to interpret the God of Israel as the universal deity and will tend to make all New Testament talk of God incar-nate seem incoherent.[23]

Here I must pause to express my exasperation with modernist sensi-bilities. The classical doctrine of *creatio ex nihilo* guides us toward a read-ing of some ambiguous words and phrases in Genesis so that we can give very straightforward and plain-sense readings of countless other biblical verses. How, then, could a rejection of this doctrine, supposedly for the sake of preserving the integrity of the biblical text, succeed on its own terms? If we set aside *creatio ex nihilo,* then I suppose we can become more intimate with a scholarly construct called Ancient Israelite religion, but we cannot read Genesis 1 without crossing our fingers on a huge number of biblical verses that suggest any form of divine presence. Of course, the very concept of Ancient Israelite religion was invented to shift the focus of in-terpretation away from what the scriptures say about God and toward something more occult and inconsequential, and therefore more easily be-lieved, which is why we never seem to notice that our approach to the Bible and its talk about God has become incoherent. It is precisely to avoid both this blindness and this incoherence that classical doctrine was developed.

Third and finally, a reading of Genesis 1 governed by the doctrine of creation *ex nihilo* helps motivate the christological maximalism that char-acterizes classical Christian interpretation of Scripture.[24] Irenaeus based his rejection of Gnostic accounts of Jesus upon a complex refutation of the Gnostic doctrine of creation.[25] The Gnostic doctrine presumed that the world in which we live is the final fruit of a cosmic evolution characterized

---

23. For a discussion of the theologically paralyzing consequences of placing God within a well-furnished metaphysical system, see William Placher, *The Domestication of Transcendence: How Modern Thinking About God Went Wrong* (Louisville: Westminster/ John Knox, 1996).

24. For the use of the term "christological maximalism" and suggestions about its im-portance in the early Christian project of forming a coherent overall interpretation of the data of Scripture and tradition, see George A. Lindbeck, *The Nature of Doctrine: Religion and Theology in a Postliberal Age* (Philadelphia: Westminster Press, 1984), pp. 92-96.

25. *Against the Heresies,* Book I.

by many layers of spiritual or supernatural reality emanating from the one transcendent and eternal deity. With a graduated ontological scheme at their disposal, Gnostic teachers were able to avoid the evident absurdity of saying that Jesus was God incarnate. They could assign to Jesus an intermediate redemptive significance. He is above us in ontological significance, and he offers a hand to pull us up to the next higher link in the great chain of being.

Irenaeus's arguments against the Gnostics amount to a case on behalf of the doctrine of creation out of nothing. The ontological parsimony implicit in *creatio ex nihilo* means that Jesus is either simply a man, or he is God incarnate. There are no other ontological alternatives. This disjunctive situation is not a narrowly christological matter. It has to do with the larger, *sola gratia* structure of so much of the Bible. St. Paul's analysis of Abraham's justification, and by extension the logic of the larger project of divine blessing, emphasizes the lack of mediating realities between God and finite reality. Upon what might Abraham rely other than God, "who gives life to the dead and calls into existence the things that do not exist" (Rom. 4:17)? All other things are "as good as dead" (4:18), and thus "no one might boast in the presence of God" (1 Cor. 1:28). The ontological parsimony entailed by *creatio ex nihilo* eliminates half-measures, and as Paul reasons, this presses us toward God alone as the power of salvation. In this way, the christology outlined by Irenaeus and developed by the later tradition simply follows from the logic of Paul's rigorous arguments for a *sola gratia* account of salvation, arguments that are themselves dependent upon a reading of Genesis 1 as teaching a creation out of nothing.

There are surely further warrants for the classical doctrine of creation out of nothing, but my goal has not been to provide an exhaustive account. Instead, I have tried to illustrate a simple point about theological exegesis. Exercising ourselves to see the concord between Scripture and doctrine does not silence Scripture. Christian doctrine is a nearly two-thousand-year-long research project into the inner cogency of the Bible. Precisely because the church has long accepted the principles of apostolic legitimacy and vitality, her teachings have been formed in order to maximize our ability to bring Scripture alive in our minds. Therefore, if we read Scripture theologically, that is to say, if we read to discern the concord between doctrine and Scripture, then we will find our exegetical judgments energized and extended across the biblical text as a whole in an integrated, continuous intellectual practice of reading and reasoning about Scripture.

III

Nothing I have said about the nature of theological interpretation contradicts the conviction that modern historical-critical study of the Bible remains a sophisticated and helpful mode of reading. Applying techniques of textual analysis such as form and redaction criticism dramatizes the diversity and complexity of the biblical text. The same holds for efforts to discern social contexts for composition and reception. I remember reading Gerd Thiessen's study of the social setting of Paul's letters to the Corinthians. Having a vivid sense of the social context liberated me from my unconscious and stultifying assumption that Paul (and all of Scripture) uttered timeless truths into the great void of eternity. To hear Paul speak to real people in an actual community did not make him seem distant and diminished. On the contrary, it made Paul's voice living and present.

For all that I have gained from historical-critical study of the Bible, however, I reject efforts to build bridges between theology and biblical studies. If the principles of apostolic legitimacy and vitality are sound, then it cannot be the case that theology can be an intellectual practice fundamentally distinct from biblical interpretation. But I want to do more than press home the conclusion to a syllogism. An analogy to scientific inquiry can help us understand the absurdity of imagining that theology and biblical study can function independently.

It may be the case that historical study of ancient myths of creation and the redaction criticism helps us see how Genesis 1 is part of a priestly, legal, and temple-oriented strand running through the Pentateuch. There are many other tools of modern analysis that may enrich and deepen our reading, literary and anthropological as well as historical and sociological. Being modern intellectuals means inheriting modern techniques of analysis, and this may magnify and clarify our vision as readers. But the crucial point is that none of these techniques of analysis can tell us what the Bible says. Scientists have experimental techniques that they use to identify and clarify data. They can add precipitants to separate compounds into their constituent elements. They can carbon-date fossils to place them in an accurate timeline. But a redoubled application of these techniques will not produce a scientific theory. An electron microscope refines our sense of what the data are — it does not interpret that data by way of its improved accuracy. The same holds for historical-critical techniques. It is simply comical to imagine that the intellectual techniques that help us bring the Bible into focus as a diverse and historical document can also double as synthetic tools for interpretation.

At this point I could go on to point out how far-fetched and allegorical are modern attempts to perform an alchemical transformation of sophisticated data analysis into some larger interpretive account. Reading Marcus Borg involves entering into occult theories of religious consciousness in which Paul Tillich is wedded to Norman O. Brown in the seventh epoch of the liberated ego as it bursts the bonds of social finitude. Even the sober Gerhard von Rad can sound positively vatic when he pronounces upon rather than reasons about theological topics in his commentary on Genesis. These unsatisfactory results are inevitable. Insofar as modern biblical studies self-consciously reject classical Christian doctrines and take up modern doctrines about religion and human consciousness (or the now popular postmodern doctrines about society and power and difference) as the organizing principles for exegesis, we will get exegesis that links Scripture to sociology or sociological doctrines (or the doctrines of French literary theory). Or we will get desperate theological gestures that, however true in themselves, fail to bring Scripture into a living relationship with church teaching.

But I do not what to focus on the speck in the eyes of modern biblical scholars. What concerns me is the beam in my own theological eye. During the Second World War, Henri de Lubac wrote a series of lectures and essays. He wanted to understand why the Christian culture of Europe was failing, why, to use his words, "the whole edifice of European civilization seems to be collapsing."[26] De Lubac had no illusions about the barbaric

---

26. *Theology in History,* trans. Anne Englund Nash (San Francisco: Ignatius Press, 1996), p. 441. Citations to follow in parentheses.

paganism of modern European ideologies, but he did not focus his attention on the enemy without. He was concerned about the enemy within. For, as he observed then, "At the root of everything, it must be said, there is a failure among Christians" (p. 441).

According to de Lubac, his failure — our failure — has a number of sources, but the most important was and remains a loss of spiritual contact with the prime substance of Christian truth, the holy scriptures. The deep source of Christian impotence in the present age, he writes, is "the renunciation of knowing and using the Bible" (p. 226). This is especially true of the Old Testament. "Many theologians," he observed, and it has remained all too true, "forego acquiring a deeper knowledge of it, considering it an obscure domain, reserved for the exploration of a few, rare specialists" (p. 226). To return to the analysis I put forward in the first section of this paper, theologians have lost sight of the principles of apostolic legitimacy and vitality. They — again, we — neither see nor seek a living relationship between doctrine and Scripture.[27]

Henri de Lubac provides a close analysis of how and why theology has become alienated from Scripture. The details are complex, but the overall assessment is straightforward. Modern theology has for too long

---

27. Any Catholic theologian serious about the recovery of Scripture as the soul of theology must come to terms with the pervasive supersession of Scripture by doctrine in so much of post-Reformation Catholic theology. It is a legacy still very much alive in the influential work of Karl Rahner. In his *Foundations of Christian Faith,* Rahner warns against "mere biblicism." According to Rahner, the old Protestant method of theology was organized along the lines of a detailed biblical theology, but now such an approach is "basically obsolete." Modern historical-critical study has sole authority to determine the content of the Bible, and an intellectually respectable dogmatic theology "can make use of only as much scriptural data as is sufficiently certain from an honest exegesis" (William V. Dych, trans. [New York: Seabury Press, 1978], p. 14). It turns out that very little scriptural data is useful for dogmatic theology, and the vast majority of Rahner's work runs on the cognitive energy of his transcendental theology in concert with appeals to official church doctrine. The upshot may be materially very different from the reactionary neo-scholasticism that animated *Humani Generis,* but his theology is formally similar. All emphasis falls on the philosophical conceptualities and their roles in framing officially defined church doctrine.

The problem of doctrinal supersession of Scripture is not a solely Catholic problem. For my own attempt to diagnose the migration of theology from Scripture to doctrine, see "Theology in the Ruins of the Church," *Pro Ecclesia* 12, no. 1 (Winter 2003): 15-36.

functioned as a perverse Christian scientism. "It is," writes John Webster, "fatally easy to prefer the relatively clean lines of doctrine to the much less manageable, untheorized material of the Bible."[28] It is easier still to dwell among the concepts of election and incarnation and perichoresis, as if they have a substantial, superluminous truth resident within themselves. This scientism, this failure to see that the purpose of doctrine and theology is to maximize the penetration of the mind into the world of Scripture, is what we must overcome.[29] The great doctrines of the church are exegetical judgments given communally authoritative form, and they are living truths for us only insofar as we enter into them through an ongoing practice of biblical interpretation. Theology is not something other than interpretation. Theology can digress into metaphysics and moral theory, into anthropology and any number of other topics. Theology is the queen of the sciences, and she has all things under her dominion. But the fundamental role of the queen is to discern the truth about God by way of interpreting his holy word, and all the different avenues of theological inquiry are for the sake of sustaining and extending the core theological project of interpretation. For this reason, we must firmly reject the self-satisfied notion that there could ever be something called theology from which or to which bridges to biblical study need to be built.

But there is a bridge we need to build. We need to see and explain how Scripture testifies to the gospel of Jesus Christ. The principle of apostolic legitimacy must hold sway. We also must have a vivid sense of how scripture gives life to the church that springs from the very same gospel. The imperative of apostolic vitality must work upon our theological imaginations.

There is neither complacency nor any sort of ecclesial triumphalism in the principle of apostolic legitimacy and imperative of apostolic vitality. On the contrary, to believe that what the church teaches and what the Bible says should be linked drives us away from the complacent doctrinalism and sterile historicism that we have tolerated for far too long. Thus, the

28. *Holy Scripture: A Dogmatic Sketch* (Cambridge: Cambridge University Press, 2003), p. 130.

29. On this imperative, see John Webster's exposition of the theological pedagogy of Zacharias Ursinus, with pointed contrasts to modern theological sensibilities, *Holy Scripture*, pp. 107-35.

bridge we now need is from where we are now — from our current awakening to the complacency and sterility of many of our inherited theological and interpretive practices — to the intellectually vibrant project of interpretation that restores a living relationship between doctrine and Scripture.

The Strange New World of the Bible

ROBERT W. JENSON

I

"Let him kiss me with the kisses of his mouth!" she says. And then she turns to him, "Draw me after you, let us make haste. . . ." As she is drawn into love so she draws the reader; the opening of the Song of Songs invites us into the world of this passionate woman and her lover.

Their world does not seem strange at first; we think we know about kisses; we think we live in the world to which kisses belong. Even if we are deprived of kisses or have for religious or other good reason renounced them, we think we know what we are missing or have given up. And indeed, at least at first, the love-world of the Song is recognizably our world of bodily longing and bliss and deprivation and the rest of it.

Yet — as the Song then leads us through its world, its familiarity becomes evasive. In the Song, the contours of love prove sharper than are the contours of our loves — did ever an earthly tryst come off quite so flawlessly as the one the woman arranges in a countryside bower amid spring's blossoms? In the Song the antinomies and conflicts of love are often bizarre: What are we to make of this woman, who — to choose but one incident — on discovering her lover missing from their bed rushes into pitch-dark Jerusalem to find him, confessing the while that she has no idea where to look, and on encountering a police patrol inquires after him in terms that guarantee they will not know whom she is talking about?

The world of the Song gradually opens as a love-world not reported, but *imagined* by a poet, a seemingly high-modernist poet devoted to strange juxtapositions and riddles with no solution — someone a bit like the poet of J. Alfred Prufrock's love song, with better luck.

And then, just as we have settled in to enjoy the poetry — or anyway what we can make of it — we come to the couplet that is usually regarded as the climax of the Song: "Love is strong as death, jealousy fierce as the grave."[1] If we ponder these lines, we will eventually have to ask: *Whose* love can such love be? Whose love can bind as absolutely as death, whose jealousy will no more give up its prey than does the grave? Whose love exactly has the Song been celebrating?

And if we are brought up short by this question, we may then notice that the language of this couplet is playing with us: that Hebrew *moth* in the first line of the couplet can indeed be translated simply "death," but is also the proper name of a Canaanite god, the enemy of the life-giving gods, that Hebrew *sheol* in the second line can indeed be translated simply "grave," but is also the name for that grasping negation of being which so many psalms beg the Lord to avert. *Whose* love and jealousy can match the god of death and the power of chaos? The couplet teases us, veiling and unveiling itself as — theology.

And we may then even remember that in one passage of Scripture, "Jealousy" is a proper name of Israel's God.[2]

What love-world is it then into which the Song's celebration of kisses finally draws us? Who now is the poet? Can this any longer be a poet like that Catullus of whose most famous lines the Song's opening may remind us?[3]

Nor are we even allowed to rest in such theological figurations, for if we read on through the Song's remaining verses, we find ourselves plowing through what is unmistakably a harassed editor's dumping ground for leftover fragments. At the end, we are brought rudely back to the earth where editors slave.

*   *   *

1. 8:6.
2. Exodus 34:14.
3. Da mi basia mille, deinde centum, deinde mille altera. . . .

Another opening.[4] Ezekiel reports: "In the thirtieth year, in the fourth month, on the fifth day of the month, as I was among the exiles by the river Chebar. . . ." He is at pains to nail down the earthly chronology and geography, and the political situation in which he finds himself — a situation of exile familiar throughout earthly history.

But then, "The heavens were opened, and I saw visions of God." More abruptly than in the Song, a new and strange world opens, the world called heaven, the part of creation that God has made for his own dwelling and in which he is seen and adored by his creatures of angels and saints, the world that would open to John on Patmos and to Dante at the climax of his journey.

And so in the proper fashion of such apocalyptic adventurers, Ezekiel sees what is to be seen in heaven, uniquely of course the heavenly throne itself and a Presence thereon, a Presence at first so sheerly other than anything on earth that its fire and beauty is said by Ezekiel to be but "the *likeness of* the *appearance of* the *glory of* God."

All very properly transcendent — except that this heavenly throne has wheels, and after its suitably spectacular appearance trundles along by that same river Chebar. As Ezekiel looks about at the environs of heaven's throne, it is after all earth that he sees under its wheels and under his own feet, the world that requires that if there are to be traveling thrones, they must have wheels, with however marvelous a four-wheel universal.

And yet another opening into a new yet not altogether discontinuous world, and this the strangest, last, and most briefly describable of my instances. When on the third day faithful women and then some of the disciples looked into the empty tomb, and one went in to check, what world beyond the entrance did they look into or indeed venture upon? It was a chamber cut into a rocky face somewhere in the vicinity of Jerusalem, the possession, it is said, of a man of earthly substance — *in which* death was swallowed up in victory, to make that hollow in the rock the very gateway of heaven. It should occasion no surprise that Mark gives us his doubly off-putting ending: the women flee and readers are frustrated. That emptiness was enough to put off the hardiest. And then again a comedown, for what

4. Ezekiel 1:1-28.

could be more banal, than the disciples' subsequent disorganization? Or indeed the disorganization of the reports?

II

It goes that way when the Bible is opened — my examples could of course be multiplied, though the empty tomb trumps all. A world opens that is at first our earth, and then is strange and new and beyond our conceptions, and then again with all its novelty and discontinuity is somehow the world we truly inhabit. The love-world opened by the Song is at once the world of earthly kisses and the world of the Lord's love for his people. The heaven that opens to Ezekiel, and that displays the eternal throne, is touring earth tending to politics. And for all we know, the rock containing the gate of heaven is perhaps still somewhere near Jerusalem, maybe even where tradition says it is.

How are we to understand the identity-in-difference and difference-in-identity of divine love and human love, heaven and earth, human-made cavern and gate of heaven? Clearly, we will not be able to read the Bible coherently without some construal of the way its strange new world is our world. I have of course stolen my title from the young Karl Barth, and that was his discovered problem when he was assigned to preach on texts he did not choose, and so to be confronted with Scripture on its own terms.

III

I think that we mostly get that construal backwards, and that *therefore* we have such troubles with the Bible. For of course we do indeed have our troubles with the Bible. The scholarship devoted to explaining it, to interpreting it, to applying it, to devising hermeneutical metatheories about it, increases exponentially and becomes ever more desperate; while in the church the Bible nevertheless becomes ever less accessible. I want to propose an explanation of this phenomenon. I think we read the relation between the strange world the Bible opens and our familiar world the wrong way around, and so are in a hopeless situation from the start.

We are socialized to suppose that the "real world" is a world outside faith's story of God with his people, outside the church doors, outside the covers of the Book, a world "out there." And we suppose that we — preachers and teachers and worshipers leaving the service — are supposed to carry good ideas from the biblical world "out" "into" this "real" world. Preparing to preach or teach from the Bible, I think I must discover the "relevance" of my text to the world out there. Writing a piece on hermeneutics, I think I must ask: What hermeneutical move will blaze the way from biblical narrative to real history? What, the devotional reader asks, can I get out of this passage for my current actual situation?

The "real" world of kisses — everyone tells us — is the world of *Sex and the City;* and it is the church's mission to bring forgiveness to that world, to console the brokenhearted, and perhaps to work for some amelioration of the chaos. The real political world — we are all socialized to suppose — is the world of Babylon *as* Babylon conceived it, a world of rulers and armies and territories; and we believers are some citizens of that world who happen to have "peace and justice issues" with it. The chamber in the rock, with its demonstrative emptiness and heavenly messengers, feels spooky to us; indeed the disciples apparently supposed that anything that emerged from it had to be a ghost. What feels solid to us is the rock itself and the stone that sealed its entry.

I have described our delusions in terms imposed on us by the particular history of the West, but the delusions are inveterate. In some terms or other, fallen humanity has always gotten reality the wrong way around; it has regularly inverted the relation between the creation's stunning new reality as it opens in the Book, and that epiphenomenon we call the real world. Abraham supposed that realistically the king's power was more to be reckoned with than was the promise, and abandoned Sarah to the harem. The last Judean kings supposed that Egypt had many divisions, and doubted that the prophets had any, whereupon the prophets mustered all Babylon's divisions against them — and Stalin repeated their mistake, to his empire's eventual undoing. The disciples feared that the risen Christ might be a dangerous illusion, but did not doubt the reality of the door with which they tried to shut fear out.

And *that* — I suggest — is why Scripture lacks force in the church, and indeed has repeatedly done so.

If we preach from Scripture or teach it or read for edification, we cannot avoid Karl Barth's experience. And then the question is: Which is the really real world? This world that opens in the texts or the one we take for "real"?

When the Bible lacks force in the church, it is regularly — from the time of the apostles to post-Christendom — because we presume that the "real" world is some other world than the one that opens in the Bible, and that what we have to do is figure out how to make the Bible effective in the putatively "real" world.

The thing is: it cannot be done. The Bible is in fact ineffective and *irrelevant* in our so-called "real" world, because the Bible does not acknowledge that our "real" world deserves the adjective.

IV

We do of course have to note that there is another possible, neatly polar, false answer. It is possible to take divine love for real — and then to take *human* love for illusion, to take the prophet for real and Babylon and Egypt for irrelevancies, to take the risen Christ for real and the cross and tomb for divine misdirection.

Many would-be Christians have done that — and indeed, *mutatis mutandis,* entire world religions. Among would-be Christians there is a pretty clear line between the church that stems from the earthly crucifixion and the bodily Resurrection — the church whose own inveterate mistake I have just been berating — and those prone to the opposite evasion, the "gnostic" evasion — if scholarship still lets me use that term.

If we proceed on the Gnostic line we will of course have eventually to drop the scriptures, or edit them, or supplement them with some new gospels or whatever — projects on which folk who have wanted to be Christian without the bother of faith have been laboring since Pentecost.

For the scriptures do not work very well as guides into a heaven that is simply an alternative to our world; and when we discover this problem, there have always been some who have looked for a more uplifting religious wisdom.

The teaching that Jesus imparted to his disciples, as the synoptic tradition preserved it, is for the most part distressingly plain. Among apostolic theologians even Paul, for all his apocalypticism, keeps harping on about church suppers and traditional morality and hairstyles and such. He will have to be edited. Maybe we can keep John, if we can just interpret him in the light of those other dominical sayings and acts that John says are not written in his book. Of course we will have to provide that material — perhaps by discovering yet again that there are gospels of what the Lord whispered to whomever, and really spiritual stories said to be recorded by this neglected apostle or that — and no doubt other titillations waiting in the sands, or waiting simply to be made up.

But if we are not to satisfy ourselves with religious imaginings, and yet also are not to repeat the church's own millennial mistake, how do we avoid both? That is, how does the Bible hang together, as it neither simply fetches us out of the familiar world into an imagined alternative, nor yet bows to our putative reality?

V

The way the Christian Bible hangs together generally is as a single christological metanarrative; and if it is not allowed to do that it does not hang together at all. The Old Testament or *Tanakh*, the Scripture of canonical Israel, was in the first century just there, most consequentially for the disciples of the Risen One and for the successors of the Pharisees. Each provided that Scripture with a second volume: rabbinic Judaism the Mishnah and the church the New Testament. Rabbinic Judaism's second volume is oral *Torah;* reading canonical Israel's Scripture back from it, Judaism reads these scriptures fundamentally as Torah. The church's second volume, the New Testament, is of a quite different character: it tells a *story,* of the Christ, with commentary and explanation. Reading canonical Israel's Scripture back from her second volume, the church reads it too as fundamentally a connected narrative.[5] Thus the *Christian* Bible, Genesis to the Apocalypse, tells the one drama of Christ's coming. If it is not allowed to do this it falls quickly apart into Hebrew Scripture and sundry traces of Christian origins, that is, disintegrates as a single book, as a *biblios*.

This narrative-christological unity of the Christian Bible is now more widely acknowledged then it was in modernity — though not of course in those precincts of academia where no unity of anything is tolerated. But if that is how Scripture hangs together lengthwise, so to speak, then I suggest that also its strange-familiar *world* must hang together christologically, that also the ontology, the reality-picture, that the Bible displays is christologically constituted. I suggest that it is in Christ that the world of divine love, the world of heaven, and of heaven's gate, as this opens in Scripture, is one with the world of human love, of earth, of the rock outside Jerusalem, as this too in its way appears in Scripture.

I suggest that all Scripture's openings to a strange world that is somehow our world are openings into the reality established by the existence of Christ, the reality of the Occupant of heaven who is a creature. He is one person, who is at once God and creature, because his one life establishes in the first place what it is to be God and what it is to be creature.

In him divine love and human love, God's heaven and God's earth, the tomb and eternal life — and so on with the all the strange world-pairings of Scripture — are one, and they are so because only as he is the one he is does either term of such pairings subsist in the first place. When he performs signs of the Kingdom the man Jesus opens heaven; and when he is buried in the tomb, God goes to earth. Without him is not made anything that is made, which does not only mean that he is an agent of creation. We are instructed that all things are made *in* him.

Put it this way, with the scholastic tradition: God is being and we are beings. And then let us be slightly more adventurous than the scholastic tradition usually is: the unity between us as beings and the being of all beings is not a general metaphysical principle but simply this Jesus, the

---

5. Thus neither rabbinic Judaism's nor the church's reading of the Old Testament/ *Tanakh* is more legitimate or original than the other.

Christ: we *are* at all just as we are in him and he in us. And so the Bible's world and this earth are one world, the world in Christ.

Every time the Bible opens a strange new world, we will understand how that strange world is nevertheless our "world" if and only if we see them as one in Christ. We have noted: if we make the Bible a collection of tales about a fanciful other world, it will have no power; and if we make the Bible a source of advice about how to get along in this world, the advice will always prove unsuitable and will again have no power. But we certainly *will* do one or the other if we do not with every glance into the book confess the Christ of Nicea and Chalcedon.

What the strange beginnings of Scripture open to us is the mystery of Christ. And our preaching and teaching and reading from Scripture will have power as — and only as — the mystery of Christ is at every biblical step what we discover in the Bible and preach and teach and obey.

VI

So who are lovers of the Song? The rabbis and the fathers of the church and the medieval and Reformation exegetes were unanimous: they are the Lord and his people, and the Christian exegetes were further unanimous that Jesus is that Lord. To be sure, our great forebears tended just a bit to what I called the Gnostic reading, often reading the human lovers right out of the story, and we should not follow them in that.

We will read the Song as the unique universal love-lyric, in which divine love and creaturely love serenade one another in canon. The love here celebrated, the preacher should say, is the love which is the very being of Christ, in whom the God who loves and we who are to love God are one body of love.

And then the preacher will invite us to enter that body, at once in the love-feast of the Eucharist and in our loves of this earth — for these too can be a "great mystery." And the preacher will proclaim the coming fulfillment in which there will no longer be a difference between them, no difference between Eucharist and created passion, the day when the church, carrying all the created loves of her members, will enter the eternal love of the Father and the Son in the Spirit.

30

*   *   *

Or what is heaven doing traveling along our rivers, as in Ezekiel's revelation? A few verses further along, Ezekiel finds a clue. The glories shift a little, and he sees that the Presence over the throne has after all a shape: it looks — somehow — like a man. We may ask why that is so. And the answer of Nicea and Chalcedon is: because when we see face to face and no longer in a glass, when we are no longer blinded by all that transcendence, we will see that the Presence *is* a man, the man Jesus who is one of the Trinity, who of eternal right appears upon the throne.

The preacher should tell us that: our brother who loved us to the end is the very content of heaven, and this is why we can entrust ourselves to heaven. Indeed, the message is more immediate. The risen Christ's presence in the church, in all its modalities, is heaven's presence. Martin Luther's favorite characterization of the church was that it is the gate of heaven: when we enter it, we enter Christ and he enters us. We enter heaven's earthly gate and earth's heavenly atrium.

Which brings us to the ultimate mystery: that gate of heaven hacked from a rock outside Jerusalem. The Resurrection of the conclusively dead one to be the final living one — that is the unity which appears in all the strange unities in Scripture. And here I will shortly cease talking, as I think exposition and explanation of Easter's world-opening should be very circumspect, should efface itself in mere service to other modes of the word.

The Bible opens twice in the church's gatherings: once read as text, without the addition of anyone's opinions or — if readers are well trained — even too much of the reader's expressivity, and then, surely after a pause, through the efforts of the preacher. Telling the *Resurrection,* the book can open heaven with little help from us. At Easter the Bible fulfills itself: the text *is* the message.

That identity is the famous hermeneutical principle for which we have spent so much time looking. At Easter, if the Bible recruits anything to its voice, it is not so much exposition and explanation as music. Once I introduced a lecture by breaking into song; I once thought it would be clever to end here that way. But I shall wait until the world comes clearly together and we are in better voice.

Sharper Than a Two-Edged Sword:
Following the Logic of the Text in Preaching

THOMAS E. BREIDENTHAL

I would like to thank my friend and neighbor in Princeton, Robert Jenson, for suggesting me as a participant for this conference, and Michael Root for inviting me. I do not teach homiletics, and I owe anything I know of a formal nature in that area to the Rev. Dr. Charles Taylor, who was my teacher at Church Divinity School of the Pacific, my seminary. So I fear it may be presumptuous of me to address you today on the topic of preaching. I was asked last evening whether I preferred lecturing or preaching. I said I enjoy both, but am not so sure I am comfortable lecturing *on* preaching. I am among you as one practitioner among many, and I am grateful for the opportunity to reflect out loud — and, I hope, with plenty of feedback — on what I take to be the essential homiletic task.

Let me begin with two confessions. First, I wish I could tell jokes in the pulpit, but I never get them right, so I've largely given up on that. Second, I have a problem with sermons that stray too far from attention to Scripture. This may be because I'm not too good at spinning narratives myself — a failing that is related, no doubt, to my ineptitude with punch lines. Nevertheless, the hunger for scriptural understanding is so great, and the time afforded to the preacher is so short, that no words should be wasted on anything that doesn't further our engagement with the text at hand. I am not interested in stories, poetry, or descriptions of visual artwork that parallel the drift of Scripture, unless, like ancient midrash, they find their source in a scriptural conundrum and loop back to Scripture as soon as they can. In addition, I object to the false distinction often made between "scriptural sermons" and "political" or "pastoral" ones: I find that sticking close to Scripture gets me more quickly to whatever political or pastoral issues need to be addressed.

Which brings me to my focus for today. It is very easy to come to Scripture having already decided what needs to be addressed. This is the case whether we are following the common lectionary or choosing the readings on our own. It takes scarcely any engagement with a passage of Scripture to come up with a summary statement of what it's all about, and to wheel off from that into a "canned" sermon, or a sermon that serves a personal or institutional agenda that isn't directly related to the text at hand. This is problematic for two reasons. On the one hand, it permits the preacher to pursue his own favorite themes, or to cater to a congregation's tastes, without being accountable to the unfamiliar or unpleasant messages with which Scripture abounds. On the other hand, such sermons sidestep the moral practice that lies at the heart of preaching, namely, placing oneself as preacher in a position to be addressed, probed, and dissected by a scriptural text, so that through one's preaching of it, the text can intrude upon God's people with grace and power.

I am referring, obviously, to Hebrews 4:12, which has provided me with the title for this lecture. "Indeed, the word of God is living and active, sharper than any two-edged sword, piercing until it divides soul from spirit, joints from marrow; it is able to judge the thoughts and intentions of the heart."

When I say that the preacher should place herself in a position to be probed and judged by the two-edged sword of the gospel — or dropping one letter, I might say the two-edged *word* of the gospel — I do not mean to imply that God's word requires anything of me to do its work, still less that I as a preacher am beyond the reach of God's word unless I present myself before it. But there is a difference between Christ the living Word who can hunt us down wherever we are, and the written word of God, which must be taken up and read. Like any text, sacred Scripture is a dead letter when it lies unread. And even when it *is* read, its meaning is a function of our interaction with it as readers who bring our own agendas and interpretive frameworks to the text. For Scripture to come alive as the word of God, we must choose to read it. We must place ourselves in a position to be addressed.

Moreover, *how* we approach the text of Scripture makes all the difference. With what attitude, with what intention do we present ourselves? Do we approach the text as something that is in our hands, as it were, or as something that, once encountered and awakened, lays hold of us?

The fact that Scripture is a dead letter apart from our attention to it suggests that Scripture is passive before our gaze, our criticism, our chosen hermeneutical approach. But it can as easily be said that the essential opaqueness of the written word lends Scripture an appearance and authority that is peculiarly analogous to the appearance and the authority of the God to whom it witnesses. The obduracy of the written word is part of its meaning for us. We could never consider Scripture to be revelatory if we were unwilling to consider as part of its revelatory character its finality and imperviousness to revision, even when it is repugnant, or inconsistent, or seemingly trivial.

A witness written down cannot be revelatory unless the medium fits the message. To have Scripture at all is to assert the adamantine character of the gospel: like the great stone cliffs of Yosemite in the photographs of Ansel Adams, the news about Christ, despite its human messiness and coherence, despite its Spirit-filled audacity and self-exposure, becomes, in written form, a reflection of Christ's own immovability, his refusal to be budged. It is actually remarkable that Christianity has adopted a canon of Scripture at all, given our uneasy relation to the written word, our founding assertion of a new, direct experience of the Spirit in Christ. We have risked the dead letter in order to preserve intact the original encounter with a Word which is not only immediate but intractable.

Does this mean that Scripture is the inerrant word of God? Yes and no. Yes, inasmuch as, when every written claim has been brought into relation to all the rest of Scripture, God's truth, to the extent that we can know it, will appear. No, inasmuch as Scripture is first and foremost a human word brought alive by human interaction with it — a human word deemed by the community of faith to be an authentic witness to the character and work of God. Because it is an authentic witness, it points truly to God. Because it is a human witness, it is marked by the particular and sometimes shortsighted perspective of the community from which it emerged and to which it was addressed. Yet since it is shot through with the Spirit, it also bears within itself the capacity for self-correction, whether through its own internal tensions or through its own connectivity to other texts, which may balance or correct it.

This in no way diminishes the authority of any given passage as the word of God. God's truth is present in Scripture the way it is present in any genuine witness; it descends to meet it and to fill it in its upward movement. For this reason every word, every nuance of diction and sequence, is saturated and overflowing with God's word. The canon of Scripture is like a vast hologram, each portion of which contains the whole message of creation, judgment, redemption, and call. If the witness is true, then what the witness points to is contained therein.

Therefore, critical engagement with Scripture is not the opposite of submission to scriptural authority. Indeed, they go hand in hand, if my initial discomfort with a passage leads me deeper into its dynamics in order to follow up its amenability to correction. As John Howard Yoder taught us long ago with regard to Ephesians 5, with all its talk of wives and slaves submitting to husbands and masters, the tug of the Spirit may subvert what causes us discomfort, but it almost always does so in such a way as to draw us further out to sea. The problem of patriarchal subordination is not solved by introducing a non-scriptural notion of egalitarianism, but by consigning all of us to a unilateral subordination to one another that leaves us all perpetually in each other's debt.

In just this way every word of Scripture is a doorway, a rabbit-hole, a magic looking-glass leading onto holy ground. Critical engagement with Scripture proceeds on the assumption and with the expectation that every complaint about a given passage will eventuate in a reversal — one in which the tables are turned and the sword is aimed back at the critic. As Paul Ricoeur famously remarked, the text reads us, revealing to us our own agendas and prejudices even as we attempt to impose them on the text.[1]

For me, then, to read Scripture is to discover, in its steady witness to the judgment and love of God, my own resistance to that judgment and that love. If I keep my resistance steadily in mind, and bend over back-

---

1. See *Time and Narrative,* vol. 1, trans. Kathleen Blamey and David Pellauer (Chicago and London: University of Chicago Press, 1984-1988), p. 71.

wards to counteract it, it is just possible that the text will manage to get the upper hand, and, like a partner leading me in a dance, will set the agenda for the conversation.

So where to begin? The work of exegesis provides the crucial starting point, although it is necessarily preliminary. Exegesis is crucial because the preacher is responsible for knowing the text as it presents itself to anyone willing to take the time to examine it. Take the story of Jesus stilling the storm (Mark 4:35-41), which I will come back to later. You remember how the disciples set out with Jesus across the Sea of Galilee. A storm arises, and the disciples are terrified. They wake Jesus up; he subdues the wind and the waves, and rebukes the disciples for their lack of faith. As I examine this or any text, I should be aware of how the story unfolds, what precedes and what follows, and who is involved. I should, as far as I am able, know how it reads in Greek, and how various words might be translated — and *are* translated in different English versions. I should be aware of textual variants if they are significant, and what parallels there are in the other Gospels.

All of this is crucial because it demonstrates fundamental respect for the text, and because any particular interpretation or spin I may take on the text should arise from and be consonant with its fundamental shape and substance. This kind of accountability also demonstrates respect for the sermon's intended audience, for they have the right to expect that what I am interpreting for them is, in fact, *this* text, considered as an object of study that each of them could approach and examine. They should be able to trace whatever I say back to this fundamental ground. Finally, since exegesis inevitably involves consulting one or more commentaries, it demonstrates respect for the wider community of preachers and scholars who have labored to see and understand the text as clearly and completely as possible before moving on to interpretation and application.

On the other hand, exegesis remains a merely *preliminary* exercise because, first of all, at least in theory, it is not yet interpretation. That much is obvious. But in the literal sense of "preliminary" it stands outside the threshold because it does not yet follow the logic of the text. The exegete is a mapper and a describer of the text, but he or she has not begun to be read *by* the text, and in that sense is not yet a reader *of* the text. To the extent that a given passage is an object to be described or a domain of knowledge to be mastered, we still stand aloof from its own logic.

How then do we cross the threshold? I think there are three ways.

The first way is the way of fascination, a readiness to be beckoned by something in the passage onto a path of study that leads we know not where. I don't mean mere curiosity, or inquisitiveness. I mean an attitude of reverence and delight in Scripture that is on the lookout for beauty and adventure because it expects to find it — like a birdwatcher heading into a wildlife preserve or a teacher taking the measure of a new class. If you love Scripture and are willing to be guided by its own logic, you will be alive to words and phrases that reach out and pull you toward them like signposts on a treasure hunt.

This happens so frequently that we hardly notice it. As we consider Mark's account of Jesus' temptation in the wilderness, we are drawn to the concluding remark: "He was with the wild beasts, and the angels ministered to him" (Mark 1:13). Suddenly we make the connection between co-existence with wild beasts, and we are in Isaiah's peaceable kingdom, and on our way to a re-examination of the meaning of wilderness for ancient Israel and for Mark. Or we are meditating on the coming of the wise men, and persistent curiosity about "frankincense and myrrh" leads us to the Song of Songs, and the bride's ecstatic announcement of Solomon's approach, his litter "coming up from the wilderness like a column of smoke, perfumed with myrrh and frankincense" (Song of Sol. 3:6). Unexpectedly, the Epiphany sermon becomes an exploration of our hunger for union with Christ. Again, as we try to imagine the paralytic being lowered through a hole in the roof into a dark interior (Matt. 9:2-8), our thoughts leap to a whole series of descents: the descent of the eternal Word into this world in the Incarnation; the descent of Christ among the dead; the descent of the Holy Spirit; and we are launched into a sermon about hitting bottom and finding Jesus there.

The second way of approaching the logic of the text is completely opposite. I will call it the way of offense. There are many occasions for us to be offended by Scripture. We are told that women are not to speak in church, that slaves are to avoid currying favor with their masters, that pearls are not to be thrown before swine, nor the children's food to the dogs, and that (as we are reminded every All Saints' Day) the faithful are to "let the praises of God be in their throat and a two-edged sword in their hand, to wreak vengeance on the nations and punishment on the peoples" (Ps. 149).

What are we to do with such troubling sentences? If we deal with them at all, we are tempted simply to denounce them or to try to explain them away. But we can do more with them than that. When Scripture offends us, it provides us with another kind of entry into the logic of the text. It does this by arresting us, by making us pause in our reading. Consider Colossians 3:22 (I quote from the King James Version, which to my mind puts the offense most baldly): "Servants, obey in all things your masters according to the flesh; not with eye-service, as men-pleasers; but in singleness of heart, fearing God." If we neither ignore nor condone this text, which stereotypes slaves as currying favor while offering no hope of release from the condition of slavery, we can still lay hold of the gospel truth that transcends such cruelty and condemns it: we are all in the condition of slaves as concerns our debt to Christ, and we are all bound to serve one another for his sake. The only way past such passages is through them, and, as often as not, the struggle to get through them takes us deep into the uncategorizable dynamics of the reign of God.

The third way is utterly passive, receiving the bestowal of meaning out of nowhere, with or without a long wait. I don't mean passive in the sense of unfocused, but rather a readiness to receive what is given. I have in mind here what Simone Weil calls "attention" in her essay "Reflections on the Right Use of School Studies with a View to the Love of God." "Attention," writes Weil, "consists of suspending our thought, leaving it detached, empty, and ready to be penetrated by the object. . . . Our thought should be empty, waiting, not seeking anything, but ready to receive in its naked truth the object that is to penetrate it" (*Waiting for God* [Harper, 1951], pp. 111-12). Applied to preaching, this means sitting with the text until it suddenly gives itself to you in a new way. I am sure there is no preacher here this morning to whom some text has not unexpectedly divulged its preachable meaning, sometimes in the hours of desperation when all hope of having anything to say had been exhausted.

To take up again Jesus' calming of the storm, three years ago I was facing Mark 4:35-41, which is the Gospel for Proper 7 in Year B in the Revised Common Lectionary. I found myself quite unable to say anything about this passage. I ended up preaching a homily about how little faith we have, and how Jesus always comes through in times of trouble. It was a singularly unhelpful sermon (I found my notes for it and that is a fair description). Last March I was going to lead a Bible study for a group of Episcopalians, and decided I'd go with the Gospel reading for that day's Daily Office. Well, it was Mark 4:35-41. As I read it over, not even remembering the earlier failed sermon, I was completely blown away by the fact that Jesus was asleep on a cushion in the stern. Not just that he was sleeping through the storm, but that he was asleep at all. Apart from the synoptic parallels, there is no other instance of Jesus asleep, anywhere in the Gospels. All I could think of was Zion's "sure repose" in John Newton's great hymn about the church: the calm, lucid sleep of one who rests securely in the hands of God. This was not the sleep of denial. It was more like the sleep of the reclining Buddha — both untroubled and completely mindful.

Now *there* is the beginning of a sermon — and it seems so obvious. But exegesis had not brought me there three years ago. In the face of my determination to churn a sermon out, and whatever blinders I may have been wearing at the time, the image of Jesus at repose in the midst of chaos was hidden from me in plain view. When I was finally ready to wait patiently for it, and when I felt no need to master the passage for my own ends, the passage simply gave itself to me. It revealed the mainspring of the logic coiled at its heart, and in so doing not only opened itself up to me, but brought me to a new awareness of Jesus resting peacefully within my own anxiety, and at the still center of my own troubled denomination. Perhaps the moral of the story is that being in a hurry to produce a sermon will never get us to the logic of the text. But I suspect that it is more a matter of approaching both the text and the preaching task with empty hands — something I find it very hard to do.

At this point allow me a brief summary. We can move in various ways from mere exegesis to engagement with the text on its own terms. I have suggested three ways. First, giving ourselves over to a word, phrase, or image that invites our attention. Second, forcing ourselves to sit with an offensive passage until we see what saving truth it points to despite itself.

Third, resting with the text with no agenda whatsoever, until the text divulges some of its treasure. In each of these cases the text takes charge, displaying an internal logic that crystallizes the meaning of the passage and holds it together in a certain way. How the text crystallizes may be different for different preachers or for the same preacher at different times. There are many ways in which the word embedded in Scripture can flash forth. But when the sermon takes its origin from such a flashing forth, then the logic of the sermon will be grounded in the word, and not in the preacher in independence from the word.

But here we encounter an irony. If the logic of the text is a word for the preacher, then the whole passage can and must be read as addressed to the preacher and organized accordingly. At the point when the text becomes a word for me, I need to allow it to follow the contours of my own spiritual terrain, and I must note the real stories and insights that this process of analysis and dissection brings to light.

When I discover Jesus asleep in the boat, this discovery immediately reveals itself as an organizing principle for the whole episode, and beyond that, for the entire Gospel. But it does so with reference to my need to encounter Jesus in repose. This image has an edge, and a sharp one at that, revealing in a flash my own fears about a sleeping God, a God who does not care, or is preoccupied, or is absent, or does not exist. I cannot think of Jesus asleep in the stern without remembering my experience as a child singing the boy soprano solo in Handel's *Elijah,* right after Elijah mocks the priests of Baal for their failure to rouse Baal to their cause. As I rehearsed, a seed of doubt was planted in my heart: What if not only Baal, but *God* was asleep? The image of Jesus asleep in the boat cuts deep, anatomizing — that is, cutting open — all my doubt, exposing everything that calls my authority and integrity as a preacher into question. I am summoned by the text to own my fear that I am alone in an impersonal universe, even as I am invited to embrace my identity as a boat with the master of the universe curled up in its hold.

For me, this experience of being probed and examined by the sharp edge of the text, however that may be in each instance — and it is different with every text and at different times of my life — is a moment of challenge for me as a follower of Christ, and a moment of relief as a preacher of the gospel. It is a challenge because I am nailed, cornered, dissected — soul from spirit, joints from marrow, fakery from truth, false sentiment from true affection, old Adam from new Adam, not I but Christ in me. But this two-edged sword is also a relief for me, because it is a word that can be preached. When the text judges me, I know the sermon is on its way, and it is going to be all right.

From that point on, the work of invention and composition has very little to do with my inner life. I have been confronted and healed by the word, and I owe it to myself to return again and again to that experience in prayer. But as far as the sermon goes, my encounter with the word is of no use unless I can shift the focus from me to the Christian journey as such. The preacher is not first and foremost a testifier but a theologian, and theological reflection is nothing other than the self-subordinating generalization of our religious experience so that everyone can see his or her own walk with Christ reflected there. Theology is a matter of plotting and graphing, sifting and sorting — a kind of two-edged sword we wield against ourselves lest we forget that the true subject of the Christian walk is not the individual believer but the church.

Obviously, then, my task as a preacher is to draw the listeners' attention to the text and keep it there. But also — and here I suspect my approach is somewhat out of fashion — I am not interested in bringing my listeners to a deeper engagement with their own journey as distinct from our common journey as the body of Christ. What I desire for them and for me is that we should all stand collectively exposed and healed by the text revealed to us as word.

What does this mean in practical terms?

First of all, I always begin with the text. Scripture is sufficiently arresting to gain anyone's attention: there is no need to sidle up to it. This is where I share what I have garnered from the work of exegesis, in as targeted and efficient way as possible, always with a view to what I intend to focus on as the sermon proceeds. My aim here is that of any teacher: to level the playing field as much as possible, so that everyone is equipped to handle the material with an equal amount of confidence and authority. This is tricky, of course, because preaching is not the same thing as teaching. Inasmuch as preaching includes teaching, it operates under far tighter constraints: less time, no opportunity for discussion, minimal freedom of movement, no props. Most importantly, preaching is part of a larger act of worship, and so is far less open-ended. So preaching the text requires a certain artfulness: a few words must suffice to bring the sermon text front and center and to get the congregation focused and on board.

Second, I proceed quickly to what I have called the logic of the text, or rather, to that point or element in the text that has provided me with my point of entry into that logic. This move may take the form of identifying a problem to be addressed (as with the instruction to slaves in Colossians), or inviting the congregation to explore a point of interest emerging from the exegesis (as in the resonance of the wise men's gifts with the Song of Solomon). Or, as in the case of the windstorm on the Sea of Galilee, it may simply be a case of stating what is obvious in hindsight: "in the midst of all the tumult, there is Jesus, asleep on a cushion in the stern." My task here is to arrange a collective encounter with the problem I have identified, or the scriptural resonance, or the presenting image, so that for my audience, as for me, that key phrase or sentence may become the sharp edge of the word. My own experience with that sharp edge informs and guides me as I set this encounter up and reflect aloud on its implications for all of us, but I bend over backwards at this point not to refer to my own experience explicitly. The goal is to sound the relevant notes of Christian teaching clearly and soon: God's service as perfect freedom; the church as the bride of Christ; the church as Christ's abode and resting-place.

Then what? When I was fresh out of seminary, my first boss, John Scannell, who is still the rector of St. Michael and All Angels in Portland, Oregon, was generous and patient enough to let me preach every other week. I'll always remember the question he would often ask me as we debriefed on Monday morning — he asked me so often it acquired a shorthand designation: YBH, meaning "Yes, but how?" Once God's word has gotten the upper hand in our lives, once our spiritual situation has been laid bare and diagnosed, once we have been offered a way forward, whether through repentance, or watchfulness, or renewed boldness in the Lord — once all that has been spoken and heard, what are the practical next steps?

Looking back, I now see that I managed to sidestep this question for years. I did not realize the extent to which I was sidestepping it, because I almost always preached within the context of the Eucharist, and so could always appeal to Communion as an occasion for renewal and recommitment. Walking from the pew to the altar rail became for me the placeholder for concretely embracing and acting on God's word in our lives. Now that I am preaching in an ecumenical chapel where Communion is celebrated only once a month, I can no longer rely on the sacrament as an excuse to climb down from the pulpit before I've finished the job. So I am very much in a mode of experimentation and learning as regards the old YBH. But I will say this much: Christian moral practices constitute the community's collective practical embrace of the gospel. We do not need to go looking for them: ministering to the weak, welcoming the stranger, loving the enemy, forbearing with one another. What I have been learning of late is that the logic of Scripture leads us straight to these things. These are not moral afterthoughts or mere practical applications. To fall before the sword of the gospel is to be raised then and there to the possibility of praxis.

I will conclude with an example. Once again, I refer to Jesus sleeping in the boat. What is this repose, we may well ask? It is Christ, enjoying the fruits of his saving work by taking his Sabbath rest in you, in me, and in all of us together. Our faith, weak as it is, our communion, brittle as it is, this little boat of a church, broken as it is, is nevertheless his resting-place, for he has claimed us as his own, he has moved in, he has declared that, leaky and ill-equipped as we are, we are his home. He is here to stay and to take his ease. The risen Christ is Christ at rest in our midst.

What is the moral of this story? If Christ is already among us in this way, then our disagreements need not and should not cause us to abandon ship or throw those who disagree with us overboard. The sword of the gospel cuts through any false integrity we may lay claim to, disintegrating us in order that we may achieve integrity on God's terms, rather than our own. This disintegration invites us to claim the true integrity of Christ among us: our fellow human beings, whether Christian or not, whether we agree with them or not about the various issues of the day, are, like us, the ones for whom Christ died. That is the message we preachers are burdened to deliver. I pray that it may be for all of us the kindest cut of all.

Entering the Story:
Teaching the Bible in the Church

ELLEN F. DAVIS

The Story as Divine Art

Some years ago, I overheard (from the other side of a thin partition) one of my students summarizing for the incoming students what they might expect to learn in my Old Testament Interpretation course. I am sure I was the only one excited by the description: "She teaches us . . . well, she teaches us how to read." That proved to be the remark that clarified my teaching vocation. I never approach the introductory Old Testament Interpretation course without remembering it, and always now I redesign the course in light of it, trying to figure out all over again what is the best way this year to teach my students how to read. At the end of this academic year just past, I saw one result of my labor — though it is, in a sense, a negative one. In a discussion about preaching, one of the students commented that she "hates it" when her pastor preaches on the Old Testament, because the treatment is "so shallow and predictable" that it offends her, now that she has some idea of the complexity of the text, of what he might have said in order to do some justice to it and to the congregation.

Although most of my teaching is not in congregations but in formal academic settings, I am working here from the conviction that we who teach in the academy and in the church share a common challenge, and by "challenge" I mean both a task and an obstacle. The task is to enable people to value the kind of complex stories we find in the Bible, and to value them in their complexity. The obstacle I would identify in our contemporary North American culture is lack of skill at reading precisely that kind of story. Among us, education proceeds largely through textbooks and information manuals, and for entertainment we turn to action novels, if we turn to books at all. We are therefore unaccustomed to and inept at handling complex stories, that is, stories that yield more and more with multiple readings, if we keep listening for the thing we do not already know.

In some instances, I dare say, the congregations with whom you work are not very familiar with the biblical story at all, except in gross outline. In other instances, there may be familiarity of a sort, but it is possible to be familiar with the Bible in the wrong way, just as you can be familiar with a person in the wrong way, and take this other for granted. With respect to the Bible, that would mean thinking you know what it says without reading it again and looking for what you do not yet know. In either case, our challenge is to enable people to have an experience of reading they may recall from childhood but likely have not had since: the experience of entering deeply into a story and being claimed by it, totally taken in — and paradoxically, it is that experience of being taken in by the story that may enable them to find a new sense of direction, however inchoate, for their lives.

Surely, if that vexed phrase, the "authority of Scripture," means anything for the church, it must point to that kind of experience. To say that Scripture is authoritative must mean something like this: through the Bible, the Holy Spirit uses words — broadly speaking, words in story form — to lay a claim on us as the people of God. The *ekklesia,* the church, is literally "called out" of our cultural confines into a larger sphere of awareness and answerability, called out in order to respond to a different kind of claim than that laid on us by our nation, our family, our professional association, our neighborhood or social class. We have been called out of Haran with Abraham, or Moab with Ruth, or Babylon with the exiles; called away from following after the sheep with Moses and David; from tending sycamore trees with Amos; called away from the tax-collector's office with Matthew. Now we have a new calling, and all the indispensable clues to it are found in the complex story, told through many voices, that is our Scripture. "*All* the indispensable clues" — I think that is what my own tradition means when it asserts (in the Presentation of a candidate for or-dination) that Scripture "contain[s] all things necessary to salvation."[1]

"In the beginning was the story," says a character created by the twentieth-century writer Isak Dinesen, whose imagination was shaped by long years in East Africa, a storytelling culture, as well as in her native Den-mark. In *The Cardinal's First Tale,* which draws heavily on the themes of Scripture and reflects light back on it, the speaking character is both priest and artist. He says: "The divine art is the story. In the beginning was the story. At the end we shall be privileged to view, and review it — and that is what is named the day of judgment."[2] Dinesen is a storyteller, not a theolo-gian; nonetheless this summation of God's work and the life of faith am-plifies my understanding of what it means to say that Scripture contains all things necessary for salvation. If indeed the story of the world is the divine art that we shall be privileged to view fully only at the end of time, then it is a life's work — the corporate lifework of the church — to learn so to read that in the end we may be found worthy to review God's *magnum opus.* We are reading (you might say) for our life. In saying that, I am reflecting on the nature of Scripture, a human witness to our life with God, inspired by the Holy Spirit with the intention that we should, by dwelling on those words, dwelling in the individual stories and the larger story they form, prepare ourselves for the fullness of life with God that we call "heaven."

In order to read any particular story well, you have to know what a story is. So I begin by identifying three misapprehensions about the nature of story that in my judgment are endemic to our culture, and all of them hinder us from entering the particular story that is the Bible. First of all, story is not information. Most of my students have come of age in an in-formation culture, not a literary culture. Although they are very intelligent and have done well in school, the concept of being "well read" has not been a goal of their previous education, in or out of school. In our culture most education now proceeds from written materials that are information- and process-oriented (textbooks, manuals, even self-help books), rather than

1. *The Book of Common Prayer,* 1979, pp. 513, 526, 538.
2. Isak Dinesen, *Last Tales* (New York: Random House, 1957), p. 24. Spelling cor-rected.

from "literature" in the classical sense (either *belles lettres* or, in some traditions, oral literature). That one fact may distinguish the most recent generation or two of (potential) readers of the Bible from all who have preceded them. It is a matter of profound importance that bears centrally on the dynamic and the aim of reading. The point of reading a textbook is not to let one's mind play over a word, a phrase, or an image, and one does not normally read such a book twice, except when preparing for an exam. Rather, a good textbook or handbook is designed for speedy mental processing, so the reader can extract the bit of information that addresses the immediate question, be it historical or theoretical, practical or personal. By contrast, a great story is meant to be heard or read slowly and repeatedly; potentially every word is worth savoring. Anyone who has read regularly to a child knows this; why do we forget it when we read and teach the Bible?

A second misapprehension: story is not reducible to plot, because the point is to provide the reader, not with diversion, but with opportunities for transformation. The extreme contrast here would be between the Bible and the airport novel. Like a textbook, the latter is read quickly — in this case, in order to find out what happens, so there is no point in reading twice or maybe in reading at all, if you saw the movie. Other more carefully crafted novels may be read more slowly, but again a reread is rare. However, there may be a more subtle distinction that sets the biblical storytellers apart from almost all modern fiction, from the kind of writing that Isak Dinesen's Cardinal calls "the literature of individuals."[3] At its best, the literature of individuals is about people with whom we can "identify," characters whose lives have dimensions similar to our own. I wonder how many of us grew up feeling that some of our best friends were in books. Although this is a very great benefit for introverted temperaments like my own, I do not think providing companionship for the nerd is the point of the biblical story. Rather for Christians the Bible is the key exemplar of "the divine art." As such it exerts upon us a certain sovereign pressure. The literature of individuals, which Dinesen describes as "a great, earnest and ambitious human *product*,"[4] may enable us to see our present situation

3. Dinesen, *Last Tales*, p. 24.
4. Dinesen, *Last Tales*, p. 24. Italics mine.

from a slightly different angle. However, it does not press for a radical change in our self-understanding, as the biblical story repeatedly does. The pressure to rethink ourselves begins no later than God's question posed in the third chapter of Genesis: "What is this that you have done?" (Gen. 3:13).

A third misapprehension about the biblical story may be the most difficult to grasp: it is not a moral tale. Its goal is transformation, and in all cases that happens through expansion of our moral vision. We grow toward God or turn about toward God as we learn to see new possibilities for human life. Yet I do not think the Bible is well designed for those who wish to draw simple moral lessons from it. It is not Aesop's *Fables.* Even less is it the book of edifying stories we used in my Episcopal Sunday school, about kids like ourselves. As best I can recall, each chapter delivered a little lesson about Christian life — "What would Jesus do?," circa 1960 — all thoroughly containable and predictable, like an episode of *Father Knows Best.* The Bible, by contrast, is a big story, restless and multidimensional. It easily eludes our grasp and says something we never imagined we would find in the Bible, or something we conveniently forgot and devoutly wish the Bible did *not* say. It takes a certain amount of foolhardiness to unleash the text amid an inexperienced group of readers and then try to field their questions and sometimes, deal with their panic.

One reason for the Bible's capacity to unsettle even its most regular readers is the fact that it is a book almost entirely without heroes. The stories of the Bible feature many people who are quite unlike ourselves in multiple respects. Generally, they have lives larger than our own, yet they are not "heroes." Certainly the people of Israel as a whole have few heroic moments. But even with respect to individuals, not many characters are consistently or even mostly admirable. Among men and women both, faulty character is the norm; think of Abraham letting Sarah go into Pharaoh's harem to save his own skin and shortly thereafter, Sarah's own cruelty to Hagar. Or think of Moses' failure to trust God that prevents him from entering the Promised Land (Num. 20), or David and his mostly vile offspring. My students are continually bringing to my attention some story that refuses to be rendered "safe" for our consumption. Recently it was the vignette about Elisha siccing two she-bears on a crowd of children who called him "Baldy" (2 Kings 2:24). My student was hoping that I could offer a sanitizing bit of scholarly expertise that would explain away the she-bears or the prophet's disproportionate revenge, but I failed to convince either of us. These are stories of people walking in the searching light of God;[5] consequently all of them are exposed for their weaknesses, their blind spots, and their God-given powers. If we commit ourselves to living with their stories over a lifetime, I believe that our moral vision and our own capacity for self-recognition will grow — but only if we refuse to be content with neat moralistic lessons.

So if the biblical story is not reducible to information, to plot, or to moral lessons, what is it that we are trying to help people find here? I often think that my life would be easier if I had a packaged answer to that question, but if I ever find such an answer, it will probably be time to turn in my dry-marker — because the teaching life, as I know it, is simply a matter of continually renewing my practices of reading the Bible, and renewing them in public. The only way I know to teach people to read the Bible is to read it myself, afresh, in their presence. When the teaching goes well, it is because I have found a way into the text that enables others to share in the indeterminacy and therefore the excitement of this particular moment of reading. We become interested in looking for something together — or maybe just looking hard, for nothing in particular, willing to be surprised by what we find. The rest of my comments here are anecdotal; I simply recount instances of my own teaching in church settings that seemed to work, highlighting the basic elements that might be worth consideration for your own work. (All my experience is in teaching from the Old Testament, but you can easily extrapolate from these instances to include New Testament teaching.)

Reading Practices

A first question with which every act of teaching begins: What shall we read, and why? I suggest that you might start with the felt need. What is the need that you and the people you serve sense in your common life, and

5. See 1 John 1:5-8.

does it point to a certain place of entry into the biblical story? This I learned from the first congregation with which I worked closely as a teacher. It was my own first year as a professor, and a parish I had not previously known asked me to guide them in a month-long study of Job. I still find the specificity of their request admirable. Why Job, I inquired? Because, the director of education answered, this parish had in the last year suffered several devastating losses by both death and desertion. They were in pain; they were bewildered; and they sensed that Job could help them with that. Even now the sureness of their instinct surprises me; these people were Episcopalians — not a group inclined to run to the Bible at the drop of a hat, and not for four weeks at a time. This was a large and exceedingly prosperous parish in midtown Manhattan, where people normally take their psychic pain to a therapist. But their choice of Job was right, and they amazed me with the steady and serious attention they gave to the text. Probably their pain contributed to the earnestness of their "conversion" to biblical study.

The next year they wanted six weeks, and this time I suggested that we continue our study with the Psalms. We started with psalms of lament, as the territory of pain had become familiar to us. Starting with the laments has now become standard practice for me, whenever I teach the Psalms. Again it is a matter of teaching in response to the felt need. Those biblical expressions of pain touch both heart and mind. People are surprised to discover so much of their own pain already written out on the pages of Scripture, and as a result they can see the Psalms, perhaps for the first time, as prayers. Praying our pain is instinctual; when we offer petitions and thanksgiving in the liturgy, don't we lead with our urgent needs? After we had worked together for a few weeks I asked them, with some trepidation, to write their own psalms of lament and also praise. And they did, these corporate lawyers and CEOs; indeed, they seemed glad that someone had asked them for a poem. The first week almost everyone wrote a lament, as do my divinity school students, whenever I give this assignment. People are more than willing to write their pain before God when a teacher gives it out on good authority that it is God's business to care.

A good reason to teach the Psalms is that they help people to locate themselves in the biblical story, since most of them are written in the first person. The superscriptions to some of the Davidic psalms help us enter the biblical story. Putting our own voices behind that "I," we take a place alongside David when, persecuted by his enemies or overwhelmed by his own sin (Ps. 51), he cries out to God. The Psalms are not narratives, but their vivid language, highly personal yet not private, is an invaluable aid in helping us align our small histories with the great story of God's people.[6]

You might also choose your starting point based on some factor outside the immediate need of your community. The first and only time I have ever organized a parish Bible study, I decided to follow the wisdom of the canon and begin at the beginning, with Genesis. The Bible as a whole has a deliberate, elegant, and satisfying order; Genesis raises and treats many of the most important matters in our life with God. Our small group of eight or ten agreed on two ground rules for our shared study: first, we would read every passage aloud, a few verses at a time, as we discussed it; second, we would keep differing "readings" on the table: a variety of translations and commentaries, Jewish and Christian, modern and classical (in this case, Calvin). I was still a graduate student, so those ground rules were not based on much experience, but the practices of reading aloud, using different translations, and letting premodern voices enter the conversation are now fundamental to all the teaching I do, in every setting. Often these provide all the fuel needed to start a discussion.

Before our first meeting that year, I had worried about when and how much to let critical biblical scholarship enter the discussion; in fact, it entered immediately and of its own accord. Reading aloud with an eye to different translations was all we needed to do. "In the beginning, God created the heavens and the earth," someone read. Another responded, "But that's not what I have! Listen [from the New Jewish Publication Society 1985 *Tanakh* translation]: 'When God began to create heaven and earth — the earth being unformed and void, with darkness over the surface of the deep and a wind from God sweeping over the water. . . .' How did they get that?"[7] Suddenly, without premeditation or planning, we

---

6. See Ellen F. Davis, *Wondrous Depth: Preaching the Old Testament* (Louisville: Westminster/John Knox, 2005), pp. 17-32.

7. Genesis 1:1 in *Tanakh, A New Translation of* The Holy Scriptures *According to the Traditional Hebrew Text* (Philadelphia: The Jewish Publication Society, 1985).

were into it, critical study of the Bible — and by that I mean, study of the Bible that takes into account the full complexity of the text, as a text. In this case, we were reckoning with the syntactical ambiguity that occurs between the first two words of the Bible, *bere'shît bara'*. (Since you need at least two words to have a full-fledged syntactical problem, that is as early as it can come.) For almost every Christian around the globe, part of the complexity of the Bible that we must always take into account is that we are reading a translated text (sometimes multiply translated, two or three languages away from the original Hebrew, Aramaic, or Greek). In other words, we are reading a text that has already been interpreted for us to a very considerable degree, because translation is the first major act of textual interpretation.

I think the single gift of contemporary scholarship that I most often hear my students acknowledge as valuable is a new translation of the Bible. Everyone who studies the Bible — indeed, everyone who is not a small child who reads the Bible or hears it read — should be aware that we are now living in an age of translations.[8] A flurry of translational activity such as we now experience is not a common event in the history of the world; the last great period of Bible translations was the Reformation. So we should recognize this for what it is, a rare gift of historical circumstance, which is to say, a gift of the Holy Spirit in our time. Two motivating factors underlie any burst of translational activity. The first is a growth spurt in linguistic competence. The archaeological discoveries of the twentieth century have given contemporary translators a philological advantage over their Reformation forebears. But the recent translation activity also reflects both renewed interest in the poetics of Scripture, the ways the biblical writers craft words, and a desire to capture that crafting in contemporary language. This latter concern points to the second motivating factor for the new translations: a sense that the text has become distant from us, that we cannot hear it speaking an urgent, unpredictable, and compelling word, the word of the Living God. The problem may be a flawed translation or simply over-familiarity with a good translation. But most often,

8. See the discussion by Harry Orlinsky, ed., *Notes on a New Translation of the Torah* (Philadelphia: The Jewish Publication Society of America, 1970), pp. 4-14.

probably, it is that aspects of our language have changed: "men" is no longer an inclusive term; "Thou" no longer feels intimate.

The availability of several excellent new translations of Torah[9] is a very good reason to begin your teaching with Genesis or Exodus. (I love teaching Leviticus, but I get to know my students before I launch into it.) Nothing so effectively freshens Scripture for my students as a translation that is at moments radically unfamiliar. Eighty years ago the great German-Jewish philosopher, Martin Buber, introduced his new German translation of the Bible to an urbane audience of German-speaking Jews. Listen to how he invites them into the experience of disorientation and renewal:

> Read the Bible as though it were something entirely unfamiliar, as though it had not been set before you ready-made. . . . Face the book with a new attitude as something new. . . . Let whatever may happen occur between yourself and it. You do not know which of its sayings and images will overwhelm and mold you. . . . But hold yourself open. Do not believe anything a priori. . . . Read aloud the words written in the book in front of you; hear the word you utter and let it reach you.[10]

Buber is asking his readers to meet the Bible as conversation partner, to invite it to speak and lend it a voice: "Read aloud the words . . . ; hear the word you utter and let it reach you." In the classroom I spend much of my time just reading the text aloud, because I know that is a gift my students will not have given themselves. Often I translate for them from the Hebrew, so they can catch the different rhythms of that language. I favor a translational style that retains a "foreign" inflection, reminding us by its word choices and usages that the English Bible is a translated text. Among the several recent translations of Torah, Everett Fox's is, to my ears, the most radically unfamiliar, while still being a wholly reliable guide into this

9. Robert Alter, *The Five Books of Moses* (New York: W. W. Norton, 2004); Everett Fox, *The Five Books of Moses* (The Schocken Bible, vol. 1; New York: Schocken Books, 1995); and Richard Elliott Friedman, *Commentary on the Torah* (San Francisco: HarperSanFrancisco, 2001).

10. Martin Buber, adapted from a lecture of 1926. Cited by Everett Fox, *The Five Books of Moses*, p. ix.

strange new world. When I use other translations, I have to check the Hebrew to see what the text "really says." With Fox, I can usually back-translate into Hebrew from the English.

Likewise, in my own translation of the book of Ruth, published as *Who Are You, My Daughter?*[11] I try to give contemporary readers something of the experience of hearing the story of Ruth in Hebrew. The translation and accompanying commentary are my fullest demonstration of the kind of reading I am advocating here: a slow reading, in which I dwell on the words and phrases of one small and exquisitely written story. It is important for me to say that I depended heavily on the insights of my students, including and especially my first-year Hebrew students, because they slowed me down enough to ponder the implications of every sentence, with its possible nuances, ambiguities, and hidden meanings. Here is one intriguing possibility: In the fourth verse of the book, when Naomi's sons "took for themselves Moabite wives," might it be important that Hebrew word order places attributive adjectives after nouns? So we know that they "took . . . wives, *nashîm*" just an instant *before* we hear the identifying adjective: "*Moaviyyot,* Moabites" (Ruth 1:4). In that moment's delay, the drama of the tale begins to unfold. For as a Moabite woman, Ruth is expressly forbidden to any Israelite man (see Deut. 7:3; 23:4-5 Heb. [3-4 Eng.]), and in the course of this story she marries two of them. Yet at the same time, "Ruth the Moabite" is the fullest human practitioner of the all-important virtue of *hesed,* covenant-love. Moreover, while the party line is that Moabites are a genealogical dead-end, Ruth is the great-grandmother of King David. So this is a quietly subversive tale that undermines the distinction between insider and outsider, between loyal Israelite and dangerous foreigner, as well as between protective man and dependent woman — since Ruth the Moabite consistently appears as the initiator, the caretaker, the one who guarantees the persistence of life, Israelite life, in the face of death.

I recently used my annotated translation of Ruth, and the twenty woodcuts by Margaret Adams Parker that appear with it, as the basis of a

---

11. Ellen F. Davis and Margaret Adams Parker, *Who Are You, My Daughter? Reading Ruth Through Image and Text* (Louisville: Westminster/John Knox, 2003).

two-day retreat for sixty women. It is rare for me to lead a retreat, so here again, I stumbled on something that I would now do deliberately, and I recommend it to you: for a retreat, choose a small story. Ruth is only 85 verses, and it has a simple structure, with just three main characters. That also was an advantage for us; in the course of two days, we came to feel we knew these three.

We focused on the question of identity, inspired by Naomi's question to Ruth when she returns from the risky encounter with Boaz on the threshing floor: "Who are you, my daughter?" (Ruth 3:16). How does one come to a fuller sense of one's own identity, in the presence of God, in the community of God's people? The central dynamic in the book is that the characters come to see themselves as blessed by God, and that happens for each one through interaction with the other two, through acts of mutual generosity, respect, loyalty — that is, through the practice of ḥesed. We focused one long session on each of the three central characters: first Naomi, then Ruth, then Boaz. At the end of our two days, someone said, "This is the first time in my whole life that I have really understood that the Old Testament is my story. This little story has drawn me into the larger story."

I think that comment is very important. Speaking now for myself, I long underestimated the little book of Ruth, just because it lacks the high drama and overt complexity of so much Old Testament narrative. Like Elijah at Horeb, I was holding out for pyrotechnics, and therefore I was deaf to the "still small voice" that is most often the sign of God's presence. Ruth is the still small voice in biblical narrative. Among the many larger-than-life characters who populate the Bible, the three people in this book are quite ordinary. They experience no miracles, have no conversations with God. But in their story, we may see something of how God works redemption through "merely human" love and faithfulness. It begins with these words: "And it happened in the days of the judges' judging . . ." (Ruth 1:1). That very first phrase signals that this personal story is unfolding in the midst of cataclysmic events of national and international proportion — and if you have read the book of Judges, you know that nothing redemptive comes from all that violence. A little later, King David's own history begins: a huge story with redemptive moments, yet full of violence and moral failure. So within and behind all that flash and squalor lies, almost hidden, this story of three people working quietly for healing within their small circle of faithfulness — and is that not how God works most of the good in our aching world? I commend to you the book of Ruth as a station of grace and sanity, a refuge for us in our own cataclysmic times.

On the retreat, our study of Ruth was deepened by the second commentary within our book, Margaret Adams Parker's commentary through images. Like my translation and verbal commentary, the twenty images represent a careful reading of the text. The arts — music, poetry, and the visual arts — have through centuries been an essential part of the interpretive conversation about the Bible in the church. So they have a place in your teaching. What kind of art should you use? Use whatever forms of art move you to slow down over the biblical story and enter into it more fully with your interpretive imagination. One thing that commends the use of visual images is the fact that many people in our culture, and especially the young, are more adept at reading images than at reading words. So capitalize on that; my students actually become more confident readers by looking at a text through the eyes of an artist. I find that I have to say very little. "What do you see here?" I ask them. And then I stand back and get ready to learn something new about the story.

For instance, consider the portrait on the opposite page of Naomi, after the deaths of all the men she loved. The line of text that accompanies it is, "And the woman was left, without her two boys and without her husband" (1:5). One of my colleagues recently taught the book of Ruth at a seminary in the mountains of Peru. When she asked the students (mostly indigenous people) what they saw in this portrait, their immediate answer was: "She looks hungry." I can no longer look at this image without remembering their insight, which turns out to echo the text itself. When Naomi returns home to Bethlehem, after so many years and so much loss, she exclaims:

> I was full when I walked away,
> but YHWH has brought me back empty. (1:21)

Naomi is empty and hungry, physically, emotionally, spiritually.

A second image (on p. 58) represents our reading of a moment in the

story that differs from the majority view. The scene is Naomi and Ruth on the road to Bethlehem, at the moment when Orpah has taken her mother-in-law's advice to go home to Moab. But Ruth protests: "Don't press me to leave you!" (Ruth 2:16). We usually think of this as a sweet moment; after all, Ruth's lines are read at weddings: "Whither thou goest, I will go. . . ." But Peggy Parker and I read tension in this scene; it is a confrontation be-

tween two strong women. The concluding line is the narrator's ambiguous statement: "And [Naomi] saw that she was determined to go with her, and she gave up speaking to her" (1:18). The narrator gives no indication that Ruth is trying to comfort Naomi, or that Naomi is glad to have Ruth share her life. So at this moment we see them in a standoff: Ruth asserting herself with those large hands, the hands that will sweep up fallen barley and wheat to save their lives, while Naomi's hand clenches her other arm in her characteristic posture of resistance.

My final suggestion about how to let the power of the biblical story loose in your church comes not from my own teaching, but from my recent observation of others, specifically those who teach children. As I said, my own Sunday school experience was fruitless, and so for years I had no positive recommendations to offer my students. I contented myself with threatening to fail them retroactively if I ever heard they were using Veggie Tales. I thought that was the nadir until I learned about the Lego Bible, which features, among other wonders, "an adorably solemn and stern Moses holding the sacred tablets of the Ten Commandments."[12] As teaching tools, these are counsels of despair. They represent the judgment that the Bible is essentially boring, that no child could possibly take an interest in the story as it really is. But recently light has dawned in my darkness. Six months ago I encountered Godly Play, and this convinces me that there is a way to draw children into the story in its real and rich complexity.

In early December I was invited into a classroom of three eight-year-olds in a very small church. It was Second Advent, and so our stories were about the prophets and the journey to Bethlehem. We sat on the floor as the teacher set forth each story both visually and verbally. She began by unrolling a colored ground-cloth, on which she placed simple wooden figures. She told the story simply, in words any of us could understand and remember, using repetitive language reminiscent of the Bible's own poetic rhythms:

". . . we are *all* on the way to Bethlehem.
"But who will show us the way?
"The prophets.
"Prophets listen to God. So they can show us the way.
"Isaiah was a prophet who listened and spoke the word of God. . . ."
(A candle is lit.) "Let us enjoy the light of the prophets."

12. See the advertisement for *The Brick Testament: The Ten Commandments* at http://www.thebricktestament.com/books/index.html.

We sat quietly for a while. Then the teacher blew out the candles, let the smoke dissipate, and a second, related scene unfolded: "Mary and Joseph are on the way to Bethlehem. They can show us the way. They have a secret. An angel came to them and said, 'Do not be afraid. . . .'"[13] When that story had been told, the teacher led us in wondering out loud: "I wonder what is the most important part of this story." "I wonder if there is any part we could leave out and not miss anything." "I wonder where you might be in this story." "I wonder what you wonder."

"I wonder. . . ." It is a generous way for an adult to address a child, for a teacher to address a fellow learner. These are not questions that require an answer; they are not direct questions at all, and in no case is there a "right answer" to be guessed. The time devoted to wondering is generous, and the atmosphere is not coercive; it opens doors for the children to enter the story as they might choose to do. Further, wondering is a generous way to speak of the story itself. "I wonder what you wonder" — thus each of us is invited to open herself toward the text and toward every other listener in the room, confident that this story holds something for all of us who give it a fresh hearing today. Wondering makes it impossible to reduce the story to a predictable moral lesson. "When the teacher truly is wondering, the children sense wonder in the air."[14]

Afterwards the children had time for their own work, and one of them came over to speak with me; offering hospitality to the guest was the work she undertook on her own initiative. She graciously asked what I taught, and to my surprise, looked interested when I told her. Emboldened, I asked, "Do you have a favorite Old Testament story?" And in a heartbeat she answered, "Oh yes, Exile!" — an answer for which I was hardly prepared. Conversing with an eight-year-old about the Babylonian Exile seemed like a steep learning curve for me, so I tried those magic words: "I wonder what is the most important thing about that story." She was ready:

13. The script is cited as it appears in Sonja M. Stewart and Jerome W. Berryman, *Young Children and Worship* (Louisville: Westminster/John Knox, 1989), pp. 139-40. Teachers may make their own adaptation, and so what I heard that day was somewhat different. Since my memory is not reliable, I use the standard language here.

14. Jerome Berryman, *Godly Play: A Way of Religious Education* (San Francisco: HarperSanFrancisco, 1991), p. 62.

"When they went into exile, they thought they were going away from God, and when they got there, they found that God was with them there, too!" Among my seminarians, I would accept that as a creditable account of exilic theology.

Since then I have watched a little more Godly Play. I am beginning to see how one story is connected to another: by geography, for instance. Abraham starts out from a city near two rivers in the desert (the rivers might be ribbons stretched out in a sandbox, or on a piece of tan cloth); in time the exiles must go to live in a city along those same rivers. Or one story is connected to another by gesture and formulaic language. Of both Noah and the prophets, it can be said: "God comes so close to him [a hand moves down close to the ground-cloth], and he is so open to God, that he knows what is important." Thus the children are learning to move imaginatively through a very complex story and see how its various parts form a whole. What impresses me about this model of engagement with the Bible is that it rests solidly on trust in the story in its complexity. It assumes that the story is big enough, rich enough to fill the gaps opened by wondering, interesting enough to engage the child without noisy animation and phony characters. This model dares to assert that the story, encountered in quiet, in liturgically ordered space and time, supported by a few simple movements and props, will speak God's word into the heart and imagination of a child. What is more, Godly Play offers a model of education that assumes the child can be entrusted with handling and telling the story. Toddlers may be invited to help the storyteller put away each wooden piece, and as they do so, to tell why they chose that one to handle. Then together they might tell the story a second time, helping each other remember what comes out of the box first, and then next, and next. Finally the children may act out the story, walking into the ark in fear and later out of it with just the beginning of hope, going to Bethlehem and feeling the weariness of the journey. Can we see what is happening here? Already, even before they can read, these children have responsibility for interpreting the biblical story and sharing it with others. I hope that I might teach long enough to find some of them in my Old Testament Interpretation class. If so, I dare say they will help me to read the biblical story more deeply. That is something to live and teach for.

BIBLIOGRAPHY FOR BIBLE STUDY

Recent translations of Torah (Genesis through Deuteronomy):

Robert Alter, *The Five Books of Moses* (New York: W. W. Norton, 2004).

Everett Fox, *The Five Books of Moses* (The Schocken Bible, vol. 1; New York: Schocken Books, 1995).

Richard Elliott Friedman, *Commentary on the Torah* (San Francisco: HarperSanFrancisco, 2001).

On the Psalms:

Eugene Peterson, *Answering God: The Psalms as Tools for Prayer* (San Francisco: HarperSanFrancisco, 1991).

On other biblical books:

John Goldingay, *Israel's Gospel* (Downers Grove, IL: InterVarsity Press, 2003). Goldingay offers a fine, subtle reading of the whole sweep of Old Testament narrative, written in the engaging style of a master teacher. This is a volume to use for frequent reference.

Ellen F. Davis, *Getting Involved with God: Rediscovering the Old Testament* (Cambridge, MA: Cowley, 2001). A collection of interpretive essays on a wide range of texts and topics, suitable for parish use.

Ellen F. Davis and Margaret Adams Parker, *Who Are You, My Daughter? Reading Ruth Through Image and Text* (Louisville: Westminster/John Knox, 2003). A new translation, with commentary and woodcuts.

On godly play:

Sonja M. Stewart and Jerome Berryman, *Young Children and Worship* (Louisville: Westminster/John Knox, 1989).

Jerome Berryman, *Godly Play: A Way of Religious Education* (San Francisco: HarperSanFrancisco, 1991).

Sonja M. Stewart, *Following Jesus: More About Young Children and Worship* (Louisville: Geneva Press, 2000).

The Lay Practice of Scripture

Amy Plantinga Pauw

I come at the lay practice of Scripture from two angles. During the week I am a professor of doctrinal theology at Louisville Presbyterian Seminary. Sunday morning finds me teaching the Bible to adults in my local Presbyterian congregation. These two settings for my practice of teaching are interactive, and sometimes I think teaching the Bible in the congregation is the most worthwhile thing I do all week! I will begin by making some general comments about my understanding of and advocacy for a lay practice of Scripture. Next, I will examine three dimensions of this practice of Scripture, with the aid of some categories that Rowan Williams uses to denote three different registers in theological discourse: the celebratory, the communicative, and the critical.

I begin with an observation that derives from both theological reflection and life in the church: the church's practices of preaching, teaching, and living the Bible are always marked by the confusions and failings of the people of God. When you are disgruntled with the current state of the church, it is easy to romanticize the practices of some past period, or to hitch yourself to an idealized version of what the church's practices should be. Dietrich Bonhoeffer reminds us that this is unhelpful, even dangerous, for the building up of the church: "Those who love their dream of a Christian community more than the Christian community itself become destroyers of that Christian community even though their personal intentions may be ever so honest, earnest, and sacrificial."[1] Though preaching, teaching, and living the Bible are central to the life of the church, there is no assumption here of ideal practices, of practices always done well, or even with good intentions. John Calvin's frank appraisal of the ordinariness of Christian preachers bears repeating: "when a puny man risen from the dust speaks in God's name, at this point we best evidence our piety and obedience toward God if we show ourselves teachable toward his minister, although he excels us in nothing."[2] Likewise with Christian attempts at hearing and living the Word. Practices are grace-filled because they are places in our ambiguous lives where God meets us, where the most important thing we can do is to show up, open to God's work in our hearts and our communities. This stress on grace is crucial, because a focus on practices in the church can tempt us to turn our gaze away from God's grace towards our own spiritual accomplishments. Practices are not merit badges, evidence of the exemplary form of our communal life. Christian practices, including the practice of Scripture, are like holding out our hand to receive the bread of life at communion. They are a communal act of faith that is at the same time a concrete acknowledgment that we are not whole, that we are not at peace, that we need healing and nourishment that we cannot provide for ourselves.

We can take refuge in God's grace even when we suspect that our current practices are mistaken and flawed. Jonathan Edwards, one of my theological heroes, puzzles over this in his Miscellany notebooks in the context of Paul's ruminations in Romans 14:6, "those who eat, eat in honor of the Lord, since they give thanks to God, while those who abstain, abstain in honor of the Lord and give thanks to God." "It is exceedingly evident," says Edwards, "that there may be true exercises of grace, a true respect to the Lord and particularly a true thankfulness that may be founded on an error, that which is not agreeable to the truth, and that the erroneous practice founded on that error may be the occasion of those true and holy exercises which are from the Spirit of

1. Dietrich Bonhoeffer, "Life Together," in *Dietrich Bonhoeffer Works*, vol. 5, ed. Geffrey B. Kelly, trans. Daniel W. Bloesch (Minneapolis: Fortress Press, 1996), p. 36.
2. John Calvin, *Institutes of the Christian Religion*, ed. John T. McNeill, trans. Ford Lewis Battles, LCC (Philadelphia: Westminster Press, 1960), 4.3.1.

God."[3] God can work grace through our mistaken, erroneous practices. God can also work grace through right practices done badly. In a prayer to God, Karl Rahner mourns "how sullenly and reluctantly" he fulfills the duty of prayer, and tells his "weak and cowardly heart to be silent," so that his mouth will "belie" his heart.[4] In our practices, we trust the Spirit to work in our sullen and reluctant hearts.

But this confidence that God's grace works through the confusions and failings of our practices does not imply that Christian malpractice is inconsequential. The generations of Americans who used the Bible to justify the practice of slavery, for example, did horrific harm to the church and to the larger society, and that harm has been long lasting. Our understanding of preaching, teaching, and living the Bible in the church has to make theological room for acknowledging that Christian practices, including the practice of Scripture, can be corrupt, and in need of radical transformation. "We have countless weaknesses," says Calvin, "and nothing in us is strong of itself or of any consequence in proving our worthiness before God. The only foundation for that holy living which constitutes genuine righteousness is to cast everything else behind us and embrace the cross and death of Christ with both hands."[5] Attention to practices should lead us to an ecclesiology of the cross, not an ecclesiology of glory.

I chose the phrase "the lay practice of Scripture" as my title because there is a common misperception that ordinary Christians perform no crucial hermeneutical work. The assumption is that the practice of Scripture is properly restricted to those with special training, and issues in products like the biblical theologian's article or the pastor's sermon. By contrast, I agree with Nicholas Lash that the "fundamental form of the Christian interpretation of scripture is the life, activity and organization of

---

3. Jonathan Edwards, *The Works of Jonathan Edwards,* vol. 20, *"The Miscellanies,"* 833-1152, ed. Amy Plantinga Pauw (New Haven: Yale University Press, 2002), p. 326 (No. 999).

4. A prayer written by Father Karl Rahner SJ for the first evening of a University Mission given by himself and his brother, Hugo. Accessed at http://themissionchurch.com/rahnerprayer.htm.

5. John Calvin, *Calvin's Ecclesiastical Advice,* trans. Mary Beaty and Benjamin W. Farley (Louisville: Westminster John Knox, 1991), p. 56.

the believing community."[6] Linguistic, historical, and theological work all have their crucial place in the church as practices that build up the body, and some Christians may be better positioned than others for this work. But the practice of Scripture in the church is finally about a communal pattern of human existence — a shared pattern that can be seen by others.

Nurturing the lay practice of Scripture requires debunking two kinds of professionalization with respect to scriptural texts. First is the "professionalization" of biblical scholarship that sees isolation from faith communities as a sign of academic rigor, and clothes technical expertise in a pretense of objectivity. The recognition among many biblical scholars of the "interested" character of their scholarship is welcome. There is the obvious point that the academic "sources" for biblical scholarship exist only because of practices of generations of believers for whom these sources are Scripture. It is a false abstraction to consider these sources historically without paying attention to their rootedness and conservation within communities of faith. But in addition, as Wayne Meeks has put it, biblical scholars are recognizing that "In telling Scripture's stories, we have involved ourselves in the telling."[7] Much of the academic interest in, say, Israelite religion or early Christianity is fueled, at least indirectly, by the impact that the religious uses of those communal texts have had on scholars' own cultural history and sensibilities. Study of Scripture is enhanced by this recognition of self-involvement.

Second is the "professionalization" of biblical interpretation within the church. Transferring the authoritative interpretation of Scripture from the monopoly of the biblical scholars to the monopoly of the clergy is also an impediment to faith formation and general exegetical understanding. The image of correct exegetical practice on this clerical model still tends to be an individual, intellectual one — symbolized by the pastor toiling away in his or her study with the aid of special training and resources and retailing the homiletical product to the laity on Sunday morning. The Reformation insight is that the church must be a place where the Word is not only

6. Nicholas Lash, *Theology on the Way to Emmaus* (Philadelphia: Fortress Press, 1986), p. 43.

7. Wayne A. Meeks, *In Search of the Early Christians: Selected Essays* (New Haven: Yale University Press, 2002), p. 258.

rightly proclaimed but also rightly heard. The laity have a larger role in the proclamation of the Word than is often acknowledged: the pulpit is not the only place in the life of the church from which the Word is proclaimed. But even the preacher's Sunday-morning proclamation is ordered to the hearing of the whole people of God. And lest we be hearers of the Word only, as James warns (James 1:23), hearing the Word is ordered to the doing of it. Hearing and doing the Word are intrinsic to the exegetical process.

Since Scripture is the text of the whole people of God, a "popular text," as Kathryn Tanner has called it, we need to go beyond a hermeneutical focus on the production of texts, whether those are academic or homiletical.[8] Instead we should look more broadly to what Wayne Meeks has called a "hermeneutics of social embodiment."[9] In worship, the interpretation of Scripture is not restricted to the sermon text. It is also embodied in the actions of the laity, in the singing, praying, kneeling, and passing the peace. Outside of worship, the interpretation of Scripture is embodied in the laity's communal acts of nurture and catechesis, peacemaking and witness. Experiment, training, and imagination are required here as much as in any other hermeneutical endeavor.

The lay practice of Scripture requires social embodiment because Christian life is, after all, a material life. When we talk about the practices of faith we are not talking about an attempt to put our bodies to the side somehow and concentrate on intellectual cognition or the inner life of the spirit. Christian practices, including the practice of interpreting Scripture, are about a way of conducting a bodily life. Practices involve gesture, posture, seeing, hearing, touching, speaking. Practices require a habituating of our bodies as well as our minds. When Itzhak Perlman picks up his violin, and you watch it become an extension of himself, you are witnessing a profound bodily habituation. Likewise with Christian practices. When Christians from Mali gather around a deathbed in the last hours of someone's life and "sing them out," that is a deep bodily habituation. It is also an act of scriptural interpretation, perhaps an exegesis of Psalm 103: "As for mor-

---

8. Kathryn Tanner, "Scripture as Popular Text," *Modern Theology* 14, no. 2 (April 1998): 279-98.

9. Wayne Meeks, "A Hermeneutics of Social Embodiment," *Harvard Theological Review* 79 (1986): 176-86.

tals, their days are like grass; . . . but the steadfast love of the Lord is from everlasting to everlasting on those who fear him." In their embodied exegesis, those African Christians affirm and incarnate their ties to an enormous community of faith also bound by those same texts, a community that stretches across space and time, far beyond the confines of a single cultural or confessional tradition. By their doing of the Word, they also create a new layer of meaning for those common texts that builds on and responds to previous readings. Because the lay practice of Scripture is rooted in bodily communal life, it is not neat or predictable. It ineluctably involves all the messiness, ambiguity, and potential for change and conflict that bodies and communities bring.

The writings of the apostle Paul exhibit both the central importance of communal embodiment of the gospel and the ambiguities of that embodiment in the lives of real communities. Paul's letters are a response to what God has done through the dying and rising again of God's Son, the Messiah. As Wayne Meeks notes, "Paul's most profound bequest to subsequent Christian discourse was his transformation of that reported event into a multipurpose metaphor with vast generative and transformative power." The story of Christ's dying and rising becomes the fundamental text that is to be interpreted in a complex variety of ways in all aspects of Christian communal existence — worship, social relations, dietary patterns, economic transactions. "When Paul writes to the various communities that he founded," Meeks insists, "it is invariably to suggest, cajole, argue, threaten, shame, and encourage those communities into behaving, in their very specific situations, in ways somehow homologous to that fundamental story."[10] Their very lives are to be an exegesis of the gospel of Jesus Christ. As Paul says to the Corinthian Christians, in their communal life they are to be "a letter of Christ . . . written not with ink but with the Spirit of the living God" (2 Cor. 3:3).

This emphasis on hearing and doing the Word implies that my Sunday school classroom is in some respects a privileged locus for scriptural interpretation. The scholar's historical and textual tools are not in

---

10. Wayne A. Meeks, *Christ Is the Question* (Louisville: Westminster/John Knox, 2006), pp. 98-99.

themselves sufficient for figuring out "what the text meant," because a degree of "empathy with the kind of communal life which 'fits' the text is necessary for full understanding." Being immersed in the larger practices of the faith creates this kind of empathy in a way that more abstracted scholarly attention to texts does not. Likewise, "what the text means" entails, in Meeks's words, "the competence to act, to use, to embody, and this capacity is also realized only in some particular social setting."[11] An interpretation of Scripture that stays in the preacher's notes or the scholar's article, or even the Sunday school classroom, has not reached its exegetical culmination. Nor is this culmination found merely in the cognitive and attitudinal shifts of readers and hearers. Both the context and the aim of interpretation are fundamentally tied up with communal ethos and practice.

At their best, scholarly and pastoral interpretations of Scripture within the Christian community are practices aimed at guiding and encouraging this larger communal practice of Scripture. But they do not specify its outcome by narrowly prescribing proper interpretive paths. Biblical scholars and pastors are the ones whose special training permits them to open up the complexity and inexhaustibility of Scripture and invite others into it. Rather than being masters of Scripture, they stand beside poets and visual artists in attempting to portray a reality that exceeds their powers of understanding and expression, but nevertheless compels them to respond.

Despite the fact that the exegesis of Scripture has to go beyond texts, textual study is crucial to the lay practice of Scripture. The aim of this study is the recovery of the Bible, in Ellen Davis's words, "as the functional center of [the church's] life, so that in all our conversations, deliberations, arguments, and programs, we are continually reoriented to the demands and the promises of the Scriptures."[12] In other words, we are seeking a way to recover the "plain sense" of the text as it has been understood in most of the church's history. As Kathryn Tanner has noted, the plain sense on this understanding is a quasi-sociological category, "part of the self-description of

---

11. Meeks, "A Hermeneutics of Social Embodiment," p. 184.

12. Ellen F. Davis and Richard B. Hays, eds., *The Art of Reading Scripture* (Grand Rapids: Eerdmans, 2003), p. 9.

the Christian community."[13] The plain sense is the meaning of the text for those who have claimed the community's creeds and traditions and mission for themselves. This is the reading of the text that makes sense for people who go from the refugee ministry meeting to Sunday school, and from Sunday school into worship.

However, the plain sense of Scripture is not always so plain, because the settled consensus of the community on the meaning of Scripture is subject to shifts and fractures. The plain sense is thus always an aspiration and a constructive task as well a sociological description. This is not surprising, because Christians are all pilgrims in the journey of making Scripture the functional center of their lives, and the way forward is often contested and unclear. The fierce American debates about the plain sense of the biblical texts concerning slavery are a good example of this confusion and contestation.[14] Articulating the plain sense of Scripture and figuring out how to embody it are ongoing hermeneutical tasks.

To understand the plain sense of Scripture in this way requires recognizing, at least implicitly, that it functions as the self-description and aspiration of *particular* Christian communities. The plain sense is inseparable from particular interpretive traditions. Those who are uneasy with the historical and cultural variabilities of communal readings of Scripture have sometimes wanted to claim the plain sense as an intrinsic feature of the text itself. Thus sometimes the plain sense is embedded in a doctrine of plenary verbal inspiration, in which the clarity of Scripture is founded on the divine oversight of the production of the text. On this view the communal reading of Scripture is not intrinsically necessary; the clarity is located in the text itself, not in the work of the Holy Spirit illumining the contemporary communities who read and wrestle with it. One theological problem with this approach to the plain sense is that if every word and every sentence of Scripture are inspired in their own right, the narrative unity of Scripture is lost, and with it, the Bible's power, through the work of the Holy Spirit, to draw readers into the whole text. It makes it possible,

13. Kathryn E. Tanner, "Theology and the Plain Sense," in *Scriptural Authority and Narrative Interpretation,* ed. Garrett Green (Philadelphia: Fortress Press, 1987), p. 60.

14. See Mark Noll, *The Civil War as a Theological Crisis* (Chapel Hill: University of North Carolina Press, 2006).

to return to the slavery example, to read the instructions to slaves in 1 Peter 2 in isolation from the reminder in Exodus 20 that we serve the Lord God who brought us out of the land of Egypt, out of the house of bondage. It is better to accept the variabilities of a communally derived plain sense of Scripture, recognizing that without the illumination of the Spirit, as Calvin insisted, the Word can do nothing.[15]

Seeking the plain sense of Scripture in community requires a prayerful, self-involving reading that asks critical questions — about the text and about ourselves. Historical criticism plays a role in articulating the plain sense of the text. Many Sunday school teachers in American churches over the last decade or so know the sinking feeling of encountering a beloved class member who has just "met Jesus again for the first time," courtesy of scholars like Marcus Borg, John Shelby Spong, or John Dominic Crossan. What is new in the work of these scholars is not so much their readings of biblical texts, which are really repristinations of nineteenth-century approaches, but their twenty-first-century genius for promotion and packaging. In each case, the rich and interwoven narratives of Scripture have been reduced to shards of historical probability, out of which is pieced together a portrait of Jesus as one variety or another of romantic hero.

Even in its more responsible forms the intrinsic temptation of the historical-critical method is genealogy, the assumption that digging down to the earliest strands of the text, or to the authorial intention or historical situation behind the text, is the key to the true meaning of the text. This tends to keep the text simply in the past, depriving Scripture of its living voice in the community, a voice calling us to repentance and transformation. So why should the lay practice of Scripture concern itself with historical criticism?

The first thing to say is that historical-critical approaches to Scripture are part of the self-understanding of many contemporary Christian communities. Historical criticism is a dimension of the "plain sense" of Scripture for them. The Bible many churches study in Sunday school and hear read in worship is a product of historical-critical work. It juxtaposes the shorter and longer endings of Mark. Its marginal notes differentiate

15. Calvin, *Institutes of the Christian Religion,* 3.2.33.

First and Second Isaiah. It is *that* text which forms the living city in which these Christians are citizens and whose language and customs they absorb and pass on. So engagement on some level with the complex historical-critical enterprise is unavoidable.

Furthermore, attention to historical-critical work can often be theologically profitable, as an aid to our continual reorientation to the demands and the promises of the scriptures. Historical-critical work must not be allowed to function as the ultimate arbiter of appropriate interpretations of Scripture in the church. But in its own way it can contribute to the building up of the body. Its most significant function is to discipline the church's urge to domesticate Scripture for its own ecclesial ends. As Karl Barth notes, "Exegesis is always a combination of taking and giving, of reading out and reading in. Thus exegesis, without which the norm [of Scripture] cannot assert itself as a norm, entails the constant danger that the Bible will be taken prisoner by the church, that its own life will be absorbed into the life of the church, that its free power will be transformed into the authority of the church, in short, that it will lose its character as a norm magisterially confronting the church. . . ."[16] Historical-critical work can help the church avoid taking the Bible prisoner by forcing a fresh recognition of the strangeness of the text, of the distance between its cultural setting and our own. Attention to historical-critical work can foster honesty and humility as we approach the necessary work of appropriating the texts for our own theological and pastoral uses. In short, a critical approach to the texts can force us to ask critical questions about ourselves and our use of the Bible.

Creedal and confessional traditions also have their place in the lay practice of discovering the "plain sense" of Scripture. We are inheritors of a long struggle to understand these texts and their implications for our worship and discipleship. It would be unwise and arrogant to bypass the hard-won insights and collected wisdom of the larger community of readers. It is the *interpreted* text that forms the touchstone of our identities as Christians, and the creedal and confessional traditions have been central

---

16. Karl Barth, *Church Dogmatics* I/1, ed. G. W. Bromiley and T. F. Torrance, 2nd ed. (Edinburgh: T. & T. Clark, 1975), p. 106.

to that interpretive tradition. So, for example, we accept the *homoousion* of the Nicene Creed as a norm for our reading of the Bible's witness to Jesus Christ, because we are part of a huge chorus of witnesses that has been pressed into reading the texts in this way in order to make sense of the grace we have received in Christ by the Holy Spirit. The creed is thus not an alien superstructure imposed on the texts of Scripture, but the result of authentic communal attempts to live into the patterns and claims of the texts themselves.[17]

Yet we do not subscribe to a creedal docetism. The formation and reception of creedal traditions was a thoroughly human, historical process, replete with political intrigue and cultural miscommunication as well as theological imagination and insight. It is a mistake to divorce creedal traditions from the social context of their production and gradual communal appropriation, to attempt to place them beyond mediation and history.

In the context of the lay practice of Scripture, it is crucial to keep the conversation between Scripture and creedal traditions open in both directions. The creeds guide our reading of Scripture, while at the same time Scripture continues to enlarge and unsettle our reading of the creeds. The Bible itself is an intricate tapestry of revisions, retellings, and reappropriations. It is a text in conversation with itself. This dialogical style should be carried into our engagements with the creedal tradition. The role of the creeds is not to force the untidy, angular texts of Scripture into a Procrustean bed of theological homogeneity. In seeking the plain sense we create space to hear the texts talk back to our theological traditions.

If the besetting temptation of the historical-critical method is genealogy, the besetting temptation associated with the creeds is evolutionism, the assumption that what is later is definitive for our faith and practice.[18] We accept the creedal tradition as an authentic development of the biblical

---

17. Raymond E. Brown's *An Introduction to the New Testament*, Anchor Bible Reference Library (New York: Doubleday, 1997), has a helpful discussion of English renderings of John 1:1. He concludes that translations that affirm that "the Word is God" are the most appropriate ones for Nicene Christians.

18. Rowan Williams has highlighted these two dangers in his essay "Historical Criticism and Sacred Text," in *Reading Texts, Seeking Wisdom: Scripture and Theology*, ed. David F. Ford and Graham Stanton (Grand Rapids: Eerdmans, 2004), pp. 217-28.

witness. But the creeds are not intended to bind or silence the multiple texts of Scripture; they place us, along with generations of fellow believers, within a common framework for continued wrestling with them in all their distinctiveness. An evolutionist understanding of the creedal traditions would say, why bother with the portrayal of Jesus in Mark when we have the more fully articulated christology of John's Gospel? Why study Esther, who made it into the canon by the skin of her teeth, when we have the rich theological reflection of Second Isaiah? Why study the Old Testament at all except as it enhances our understanding of the New Testament? An important dimension of the lay practice of Scripture is to create space for each text to be heard. Part of that hearing will be to note the text's unfinished business, the places that seem to invite a response, a retelling. But part of our receptivity to Scripture is to listen to each part in its own right, for the distinctive word that it brings to the community of faith. We are not to stop reading the covenant code of Exodus because of the revisioning we find in Deuteronomy. We are not to stop reading the prophets on their own terms because of their appropriation in Matthew's Gospel.

Resisting this evolutionist pressure in our reading of Scripture also raises critical questions about the function of the creeds themselves. We have to acknowledge that not all readings of Scripture guided by the creeds have been helpful. The Nicene and Chalcedonian creeds, for example, make no mention of the fact that God is the God of Israel. This has encouraged a tendency to canonical readings that leap straight from the fall into sin in Genesis 3 to the New Testament, on the assumption that nothing in between has much light to shed on God's activity "for us human beings and for our salvation."[19] We have come to see in the West how devastating that trajectory away from the God of Israel has been. In appropriating the Creed we must now speak where the creedal tradition is silent.

Implicit in our discussion so far is that part of the hermeneutical context of the lay practice of Scripture is the conviction that our "context is always more than the social-ideological matrix." Both the text and the

---

19. See this argument in Kendall Soulen, *The God of Israel and Christian Theology* (Minneapolis: Fortress Press, 1996).

reader are, in Rowan Williams's words, "responding to a gift, an address or a summons not derived from the totality of the empirical environment."[20] Neither the text nor the readers of Scripture control or confine that divine gift. In our reading we put ourselves at the disposal of that gifting presence. Our aim in the communal reading of Scripture, as James Alison has said in the context of reflections on Romans 1, is to give glory to God and to create "merciful meaning for our sisters and brothers as we come to be possessed by the Spirit" of the crucified and risen Jesus. A proper reading of Scripture will push us toward "undoing our violent and evil ways of relating to each other," and show us "how together to enter into the way of penitence and peace."[21]

I turn now to a kind of typology for understanding different dimensions of the practice of Scripture in the church. In the preface to his collection of essays titled *On Christian Theology,* Rowan Williams distinguishes three different styles of theological reflection. Theology, he says, "begins as a celebratory phenomenon." You can see this style in the language of hymns and liturgy, as well as some forms of doctrinal theology, as Christians explore the fullness of faith's vision through the linkages of thought and images.[22] But by itself, Williams warns, the celebratory mode can become sealed in on itself, losing its ability to engage and be renewed by the concrete historical discourses of its environment. Thus the need for a communicative style of theology, which witnesses "to the gospel's capacity for being at home in more than one cultural environment." The communicative style dares to take "long and exotic detour[s] through strange idioms and structures of thought," hopeful that "the unfamiliar idiom may uncover aspects of the deposit of belief hitherto unexamined."[23] This in turn leads to the critical style of theology, which asks, "is what is emerging actually identical or at least continuous with what has been believed and articulated?" Critical theology is theology "alert to its own inner tensions or irresolutions," challenging and testing the church's

20. Williams, "Historical Criticism and Sacred Text," p. 224.

21. James Alison, "'But the Bible says . . .'? A Catholic Reading of Romans 1," accessed at http://www.jamesalison.co.uk/eng15.html.

22. Rowan Williams, *On Christian Theology* (Oxford: Blackwell, 2000), p. xiv.

23. Williams, *On Christian Theology,* p. xiv.

language, unsettling the assumption of "a stable and unproblematic" Christian native tongue.[24]

I am adapting this schema of celebratory, communicative, and critical styles of theology to think about the different but interrelated ways in which the Bible functions in the church. As will become clear, these three styles are not in a hierarchical relation to each other, with one kind serving as the goal or model for the rest. All three sorts are crucial to both a lay practice of Scripture and the general health of the church.

First the celebratory. A significant component of teaching the Bible in the church is to help people become more engaged in worship. In many churches, scriptural verses infuse the liturgy from the call to worship to the hymns to the celebration of the Eucharist to the benediction. But it cannot be assumed anymore that the Scripture read and sung and proclaimed in worship will be familiar to the people in the congregation, that it will tap into a fund of biblical knowledge and exegetical curiosity, that it will conform to and reinforce well-worn grooves in congregants' own devotional lives. Scripture has become a foreign language for lots of American Christians, and worship suffers as a result. Becoming acquainted, or reacquainted, with the texts of Scripture is crucial for full participation in worship.

The celebratory style illuminates the lay practice of Scripture as both an intentional, communal response to God's mysterious and uninvited initiative in our lives and a gateway into deeper communion with God. In our celebratory practice of Scripture we respond by glorifying God, that is, reflecting back just a little bit of the love, beauty, and justice that God is. In my own confessional tradition, psalm singing is an excellent example of this celebratory response. We sing the words of Scripture as an offering to God, trusting that the Holy Spirit helps us in our weakness. The liturgy of the Eucharist is perhaps the clearest place where the celebratory practice of Scripture is also a gateway to deeper communion with God. There the biblical promises of our union with Christ become enfleshed in our eating, drinking, and remembering.

It is crucial that the celebratory practice of Scripture keep its focus on praise and communion with God. The deadly alternative is utilitarian

24. Williams, *On Christian Theology*, pp. xiv-xv.

worship, in which the praise of God is not an end in itself, but an instrument in service of some noble Christian agenda: gearing ourselves up for mission to the world, or strengthening our identity as resident aliens in a corrupt culture. It should be noted that hymns are often better at avoiding this temptation to utilitarian worship than sermons are. The celebratory mode of the practice of Scripture reminds us that the worship of God is not a merely instrumental good. Glorifying God is what we are made for. "Now unto the King eternal, immortal, invisible, to the only wise God — be honor and glory, forever and ever. Amen" (1 Tim. 1:17).

The communicative practice of Scripture counters the tendency of the celebratory to close in on itself, to be content to function within an insular, self-sufficient community. The communicative practices of the church resist the temptation to what Karl Barth calls "pious egocentricity." The gospel is not to be treated as an "indescribably magnificent private good fortune" bestowed on a fortunate few for their own benefit.[25] By contrast, according to Barth, the church exists for the world, not for itself. One of the church's central tasks is witness. In its witness, the church discovers that the gospel is inherently communicable, because it is an incarnational gospel, able to take on flesh and make itself at home in a myriad of cultural settings.

As missiologist Andrew Walls notes, "the very words of Christ himself were transmitted in translated form in the earliest documents we have, a fact surely inseparable from the conviction that in Christ, God's own self was translated into human form." The world of Scripture is not a self-contained world. The story of Christianity is one of repeated creative interactions with "new cultures, with different systems of thought and different patterns of tradition."[26] Walls is not advocating a reductionist translation of Scripture into ethical or doctrinal principles, or paradigmatic religious experiences. But he is recognizing that all our readings of Scripture are culturally inflected and therefore partial. Texts of Scripture that are dormant in one cultural setting spring to life in another. Those outside the Christian

25. Barth, *Church Dogmatics* IV/3.1, ed. G. W. Bromiley (Edinburgh: T. & T. Clark, 1961), pp. 567-68.
26. Andrew F. Walls, *The Cross-Cultural Process in Christian History: Studies in the Transmission and Appropriation of Faith* (Maryknoll, NY: Orbis Books, 2002), pp. 29, 30.

community often have valuable insights into the community's texts. Christianity is an essentially vernacular faith, and so communicative practices are at the heart of the church's existence.

Walls notes that there seems to be "some inherent fragility, some built-in vulnerability" implied in this interacting, incarnational faith. Christianity's expansion has generally been serial, not progressive. The faith advances, but it also recedes. Think, for example, of churches in northern Africa, whose Greek- and Latin- and indigenous-language communities were for centuries the heartland of Christianity. Furthermore, the pattern has been that "the recessions typically take place in the Christian heartlands, in the areas of greatest Christian strength and influence, . . . while the advances typically take place at or beyond its periphery." As Walls concludes, "Christian faith must go on being translated, must continually enter into vernacular culture and interact with it, or it withers and fades."[27]

This raises some interesting questions for the church's communicative practice of Scripture. It implies first of all that our attempts to communicate the gospel in non-Christian settings are important not only for the people we reach, but for the vitality of the church's faith itself. Our communicative efforts promise to uncover new aspects of the faith we claim. But it is also clear that the church's geographical center of gravity has shifted away from the American heartlands to the burgeoning churches of the global south. The lay practice of Scripture is exploding around the world; I worry that American Christians are impoverished in their readings of Scripture because of their isolation from these major shifts. As Kwame Bediako notes, "the conditions of Africa are taking Christian theology into new areas of life, where Western theology has no answers, because it has no questions."[28]

The communicative practice of Scripture points to the dangers of settling for a parochial plain sense. It is desirable to have the members of a congregation study the Bible together, across differences of age, gender,

27. Walls, *The Cross-Cultural Process*, p. 29.
28. Kwame Bediako, "A Half Century of African Christian Thought," *Journal of African Christian Thought* (June 2000): 11.

class, culture, and race. But the fact is that congregations tend for the most part to be homogeneous communities of the like-minded. Bible study in communities of the like-minded has its place. But it does not bear the same gracious promise of broadening our biblical horizons and correcting our misreadings. Whether the topic is wealth and poverty or the place of gay and lesbian Christians in the church, the Bible's teaching about contentious issues seems so clear when you can just get those who disagree with you to go away!

A parochial plain sense is also a danger for the established churches of the West and East as a whole, when they content themselves with recovering and restoring their own scriptural heritage. There is much to be gained of course, in recovering our own creedal and exegetical heritage, and it is no small task. But this task should not be undertaken on the implicit assumption that all that is needed for preaching, teaching, and living the Bible faithfully can be found in our own backyard, and that our brothers and sisters in the global south have nothing to contribute. Isolation from the larger contemporary reality of the lay practice of Scripture also impoverishes attempts to retrieve our own heritage, as it impedes our recognition of the extent to which the treasures of this heritage are themselves the result of daring cultural translations and assimilations.

This brings us finally to the critical practice of Scripture, whose role, in Rowan Williams's words, is to challenge and test "the language of celebration, or even the language of communication when this latter takes for granted a stable and unproblematic native tongue, never unsettled by the enterprise of translation."[29] If the communicative practice of Scripture is predicated on what Andrew Walls called the "indigenous principle," the ability of Scripture to make its home in a culture, the critical practice of Scripture is predicated on what he calls the "pilgrim principle," the way the Bible loosens people from their culture by criticizing and correcting it.[30] This criticism and correction extends to the culture of the church, not only to the culture of the larger society.

---

29. Williams, *On Christian Theology,* p. xv.

30. Andrew F. Walls, *The Missionary Movement in Christian Culture: Studies in the Transmission of Faith* (Maryknoll, NY: Orbis Books, 2001), pp. 7-9.

We have already flagged the danger of an ecclesiology of glory, a doctrine of the church that is loath to admit weakness or shame. Theological discussions of Christian practices sometimes paint an idealized picture of exemplary communal practices perfectly aligned with pious intentions and correct theological construals. The concrete history of Christian practices looks very different. It is an ambiguous history, marked by countless examples of good practices done for bad reasons, of once-vibrant practices becoming confused and sinful, of communal practices becoming so strong that they dominate the conceptual space, degenerating into an unreflective "but we've always done it this way" mentality. The idealized picture of Christian practices glosses over issues of power: how decisions about communal practices are made and who benefits, and the complex ways in which spiritual practices both resist and accommodate prevailing cultural norms.

Christian practices, including the practice of Scripture, are at the heart of knowing God and forming Christian character. This is why it is crucial to embrace the critical moment in our practice of Scripture. When our practice of Scripture is healthy, it will exert critical leverage on our customary ways of reading Scripture. As Ellen Davis notes, "Whenever we pick up the Bible, read it, put it down, and say, 'That's just what I thought,' we are probably in trouble."[31] When done correctly, the critical practice of Scripture leads not to despair or cynicism, but to a humble yet hopeful journeying with the Bible.

The images of pilgrim and journey remind us that we are not at the final stage of Christian formation in our attempts to preach, teach, and live the Bible. "Others," says Walls, "will look at us and see, perhaps with wonder, our incompleteness."[32] This incompleteness cannot be remedied simply by more concerted effort on our part, but only by placing ourselves alongside all of our fellow believers, including those yet to be. God's promise is that believers of different times, places, and cultural backgrounds are to become parts of a single body, not through a cultural homogenization of their practices, but through a common grounding in Christ, whose hu-

31. Davis, *The Art of Reading Scripture*, p. 16.
32. Walls, *The Cross-Cultural Process*, p. 73.

manity affirms all of humanity. Each part of the body of Christ retains its distinctiveness, yet needs the others for completeness and maturity. Alluding to Ephesians 4:13, Walls declares,

> Only in Christ does completion, fullness, dwell. And Christ's completion, as we have seen, comes from all humanity, from the translation of the life of Jesus into the lifeways of all the world's cultures and subcultures through history. None of us can reach Christ's completeness on our own. We need each other's vision to correct, enlarge, and focus our own; only together are we complete in Christ.[33]

The whole company of the faithful is bound together as part of a single story. As we preach, teach, and live the Bible, we remember that no part of the story, and certainly no single telling of the story, will ever be complete in itself.[34]

33. Walls, *The Cross-Cultural Process,* p. 79.
34. Walls, *The Cross-Cultural Process,* p. 73.

Reading the Bible with Eyes of Faith: Theological Exegesis from the Perspective of Biblical Studies

RICHARD B. HAYS

I. "Can You See Anything?" Seeking Restored Vision

The title of this lecture is "Reading the Bible with Eyes of Faith" — a title proposed not by me but by the organizers of this conference. This title serendipitously provides an occasion to recall and celebrate the work of Paul Minear, the extraordinary biblical theologian who reached his 100th birthday earlier this year. It has now been exactly sixty years since Minear, who taught NT for many years at Yale Divinity School, published a challenging programmatic book titled *Eyes of Faith: A Study in the Biblical Point of View*.[1] At the heart of Minear's work lies one luminous insight: what we ordinarily take to be "real" is in fact a distorted picture of the world, and it is only the revelatory power of God's word that casts a true light on the landscape of human experience and, at the same time, heals our capacity to *see*.

Minear prefaces his work with an epigraph from William Blake that describes the eyes, the human organs of vision, as "dim windows":

---

1. P. S. Minear, *Eyes of Faith: A Study in the Biblical Point of View* (Philadelphia: Westminster, 1946). Minear explains that his intent in this work is "not to construct a Biblical theology, but to provide a preface for such theology by charting its context of presuppositions, those axiomatic attitudes and convictions that lie so deep that they are taken for granted" (pp. 1-2). That is to say, he is offering a prolegomenon that outlines the epistemological preconditions for composing a biblical theology.

This Life's dim windows of the Soul
Distorts the Heavens from Pole to Pole,
And leads you to Believe a Lie
When you see with, not through, the Eye.

One could take Blake's verse as an invitation to embrace Gnosticism or perhaps Plato's allegory of the cave — an invitation, that is, to renounce sensory experience in favor of some ethereal realm of ideas. Minear, however, has something quite different in mind: when he speaks of what we see through "eyes of faith," he refers to the very concrete and radically disturbing vision of embodied reality offered us by the biblical narrators, and by the prophets and apostles. In this vision of the world, the truth about human life is given only in Scripture — that is to say, only through the mysterious working of God in the election of Israel and the death and resurrection of Jesus. It is no accident, then, that the epigraph to the final chapter of Minear's book is drawn not from Blake, but from Karl Barth's commentary on Romans; Minear's approach to biblical theology is deeply shaped by Barth's radical call for all our perceptions to be interrogated and reshaped by the Word of God as disclosed in Jesus Christ.[2]

The image of "eyes of faith" as the epistemological precondition for grasping the surprising truth about the real world serves well as an entry point to our reflections about biblical hermeneutics and "theological exegesis." Minear's visual imagery might well remind us of a distinctive story in Mark's Gospel, in which Jesus performs a peculiar two-stage healing of a blind man at Bethsaida (Mark 8:22-26).[3] After putting saliva on the blind man's eyes and laying hands on him, Jesus asks, "Can you see anything?" The man replies, "I can see people, but they look like trees walking around." Then, Mark tells us, Jesus laid hands a second time on the man's eyes, "and he looked intently" (interestingly the verb is διέβλεψεν — in light of Blake's poem, I am tempted to translate it "he looked *through* the

---

2. See, for Minear's later assessment of Barth's significance, his article, "Barth's Commentary on the Romans, 1922-1972, or Karl Barth vs. the Exegetes," in *Footnotes to a Theology: The Karl Barth Colloquium of 1972*, ed. H. M. Rumscheidt (The Corporation for the Publication of Academic Studies in Religion in Canada, 1974), pp. 8-29.

3. Interestingly, nowhere in his book does Minear refer to this story.

eyes") and "his sight was restored, and he saw everything clearly." I fear that most of the time, even if we have been touched by Jesus, when we biblical scholars look at the text of Scripture, we see trees walking. (Or perhaps in some cases, we see trees chopped down, split, and stacked into piles of firewood.) It is my devout hope, however, that we are entering a new historical moment in which we will again be touched by Jesus so as to find our sight clarified.

II. Blurry Vision, Diverging Roads

Such a clarification of sight is urgently necessary, for the past two centuries of critical study of the Bible have brought us to a fork in the road, and we need to be able to read the road signs before us. The Finnish NT scholar Heikki Räisänen describes the diverging paths as follows:

> Biblical scholars will soon find themselves at a crossroads. Will they remain guardians of cherished confessional traditions, anxious to provide modern man with whatever normative guidance they still manage to squeeze out of the sacred texts? Or will they follow those pioneering theologians . . . fearlessly reflecting on the biblical material from a truly ecumenical, global point of view?[4]

With the choice so described, it is not hard to see where Räisänen's own sympathies lie. He is convinced that "the absolutizing interpretation given by the early Christians to the 'Christ event'" was "somewhat exaggerated,"[5] and that the duty of "serious scholarship" is to render a purely historical account of the biblical texts. As a result, the older project of "NT theology" should be replaced by two different projects: (1) the writing of "a history of early Christian thought" from a dispassionate neutral perspective;[6] and (2)

4. H. Räisänen, *Beyond New Testament Theology*, 2nd ed. (London: SCM, 2000), p. 209.
5. Räisänen, *Beyond New Testament Theology*, p. 202.
6. This was, of course, already proposed incisively by William Wrede in 1897. Räisänen explicitly describes his own constructive proposals as a return to the critical program of Wrede and the *religionsgeschichtliche Schule*.

critical reflection on the NT and its history of influence, from a philosophical perspective informed by modern awareness of religious pluralism.[7] Räisänen bemoans the fact that for more than a hundred years the truly historical project of NT interpretation got sidetracked by the influence of confessional neo-orthodox theology, because of the influence of Barth and Bultmann. But now at last in the bright new world come of age, NT scholarship can be liberated to move forward to a purely historical interpretation (following those fearless pioneers who approach the Bible from a "global point of view," whatever that might mean) and to leave behind the constraints of dogma. If all this sounds eerily reminiscent of the nineteenth century, that is because it is.

At least in Räisänen's case, he clearly recognizes the nineteenth-century intellectual sources of his proposal, and he understands that he is making a revisionary proposal against the grain of a long tradition of significant theological inquiry. But alas, it is not always so among members of the biblical guild, especially in the United States. Whereas a generation ago it was widely accepted that there could be a fruitful synthesis of historical and theological inquiry in biblical studies, this claim is increasingly challenged by some insistent voices that seek to exclude any sort of explicitly religious or theological perspective from a place at the table in scholarly study of the Bible. A couple of months ago, an article was posted on the Society of Biblical Literature website by Michael V. Fox, a professor of Hebrew Bible at the University of Wisconsin. In this essay, Fox forcefully argues that "faith-based study" has no place in biblical scholarship: "Faith-based study . . . can dip into Bible scholarship for its own purposes, but cannot contribute to it." Fox continues with the following disdainful remarks: "Trained scholars quickly learn to recognize which authors and publications are governed by faith and tend to set them aside, not out of prejudice but out of an awareness that they are irrelevant to the scholarly enterprise. Sometimes it is worthwhile to go through a faith-motivated publication and pick out the wheat from the chaff, but time is limited."[8]

7. Räisänen, *Beyond New Testament Theology,* p. 8 *et passim.*
8. M. V. Fox, "Bible Scholarship and Faith-Based Study: My View," *SBL Forum* (http://www.sbl-site.org/Article.aspx?ArticleId=490).

RICHARD B. HAYS

Lest it be thought that Räisänen and Fox represent marginal, idio-
syncratic perspectives, I place in evidence the presidential address given by
Wayne Meeks in Barcelona at the 2004 meeting of the Studiorum Novi
Testamenti Societas, the major international society of NT scholars. In this
lecture, revealingly titled, "Why Study the New Testament?" Meeks con-
tends that the traditional theological approach to interpretation has a
baleful effect because it seeks to find "normative" meanings in texts. The
student of the NT should now instead seek to trace the "formative" effects
of the NT, i.e., its influence on the formation of culture. Meeks does con-
cede that biblical scholars may continue to speak to "the whole unruly as-
sortment of faith communities for whom the documents we are interested
in are construed as part of sacred scripture." He even generously remarks
that there is "no reason to be embarrassed about the proprietary claim that
these groups make on *us*."[9] Still, our "largest audience" is "the *non-
Christian* majority of the world," and addressing that audience is "the most
exciting and certainly the most important challenge we will face in the
present century."[10]

The fantasy that the vast non-Christian world will have more than a
slight passing interest in the scholarly deliberations of the SNTS is perhaps
a forgivable foible of a superb scholar who has carved out a distinguished
career at Yale in a secular department of Religious Studies. What is of more
concern, however, is that Meeks's desiderata for the future trajectory of NT
scholarship include not only the challenge to address the non-Christian
world but also the assertion that NT scholars should abandon their role as
teachers of the church. He puts his case like this: "We should start by eras-
ing from our vocabulary the terms 'biblical theology' and, even more urgently, 'New Testament theology.' Whatever positive contributions these
concepts may have made in the conversation since Gabler, we have come to
a time when they can only blinker understanding." This is so because these
terms "smuggle in a cognivist model of religion"[11] and because they "claim

9. W. A. Meeks, "Why Study the New Testament?" *NTS* 51 (2005): 155-70. Citation
from p. 167, emphasis added. The firm distinction between "these groups" and "us" elo-
quently discloses the author's hermeneutical location.
10. Meeks, "Why Study the New Testament?" pp. 168-69, emphasis in original.
11. Here, as in Räisänen, we see the continuing influence of the *religionsgeschichtliche*

textual and historical warrants" for normative propositions that are actually contingent products of the interests of later interpretive communities. And finally, Meeks declares, "'biblical theology' has functioned ideologically in the attempt to secure our own positions in the theological hierarchy, as the teachers of the teachers of the church. We have not done very well in that role, and we should give it up."[12] To which I can only reply, "You have said so."

If that is the view from the chair of the SNTS presidency, how does the future of biblical scholarship look from lower down the academic food chain? I take you back now to an even more recent posting on the SBL website, this time an article by Hector Avalos of Iowa State University, titled "The Ideology of the Society of Biblical Literature and the Demise of an Academic Profession."[13] Avalos sweepingly describes "the ever-growing irrelevance of biblical studies in academia" and opines that "Keeping biblical scholars employed, despite their irrelevance to anyone outside of faith communities, is the main mission of the SBL." This is, however, a doomed enterprise, because "the Bible has no intrinsic value or merit. Its value is a social construct, and the SBL is the agent of an elite class that wishes to retain its own value and employment by fostering the idea that biblical studies should matter." Avalos goes on, "in the interest of self-disclosure" to describe himself as a "secular humanist" and to admit that even though he loves studying the Bible (a surprising statement not corroborated by anything else in his essay), "my conscience is increasingly telling me to do something more beneficial for humanity." Again, you have said so.

Here is the point I am leading to. There is an important sense in which Avalos is correct: the intense academic study of the Bible really is *not* important outside of faith communities. Once one starts down the fork in the road to which Räisänen, Fox, and Meeks beckon the scholarly guild, one ultimately, inevitably, arrives at the dead-end portrayed in

---

Schule, which sought to give priority to the lived experience of religious communities over expressions of thought and doctrine. In view of the actual importance of "cognitive" teaching in Christian communities in history, the dichotomy may be less than illuminating for the study of the NT and early Christianity.

12. Meeks, "Why Study the New Testament?" pp. 167-68.

13. http://www.sbl-site.org/Article.aspx?ArticleId=520.

Avalos's gloomy postcard from Ames, Iowa. (Were I to suggest a more concise title for his essay, I might call it "Aimless in Ames.") Once one has arrived at this destination, the very project of studying something called the Bible becomes intellectually incoherent. As Robert Jenson has incisively remarked, "outside the church, no such entity as the Christian Bible has any reason to exist." The Bible is a collection of documents gathered by and for the church to aid in preserving and proclaiming the church's message. Therefore, "The question, after all, is not whether churchly reading of Scripture is justified; the question is, what could possibly justify any other?"[14]

Precisely because the dead-end character of secularistic study of the Bible has become increasingly apparent, many thoughtful interpreters have begun to explore the other fork in the road. I am happy to say that the past ten years have witnessed an extraordinary resurgence of interest in theological exegesis of Scripture, and that several fascinating new projects are in the early stages of development. One noteworthy component of many of these initiatives has been a sustained effort to recover a sympathetic understanding of the church's ancient traditions of scriptural interpretation. Time would fail me to tell of these initiatives; in any case, many of you here are well aware of these developments, and we have been hearing about them in other lectures over the past few days.[15] A great deal of

14. R. W. Jenson, "Scripture's Authority in the Church," in *The Art of Reading Scripture,* ed. E. F. Davis and R. B. Hays (Grand Rapids: Eerdmans, 2003), pp. 27-37. Quotations from pp. 27, 29.

15. As examples of the growing interest in theological exegesis, I would draw attention particularly to the work of scholars such as Brevard Childs, Stephen Fowl, Francis Watson, N. T. Wright, Christopher Seitz, R. W. L. Moberly, Ellen Davis, Douglas Harink, Karl Donfried, and Markus Bockmuehl. Noteworthy also are programmatic initiatives such as the Scripture Project at the Center of Theological Inquiry in Princeton and the Scripture and Hermeneutics Seminar in the UK. One barometer of this resurgence of theological exegesis is the growing number of significant journals, commentary series, and other publication initiatives that are serving as conduits for these fresh streams of thought; see, for example, *Pro Ecclesia, The Journal for Theological Interpretation, Ex Auditu,* Horizons in Biblical Theology, the Brazos Theological Commentary on the Bible, the Two Horizons Commentary, the (older) Interpretation Commentaries series, Baker Academic's new series Studies in Theological Interpretation, the *Dictionary of Theological Interpretation of the Bible,* The Ancient Christian Commentary on Scripture, and The Church's Bible. For some particularly

scholarly energy is now being poured into theological exegesis. The initial results of these efforts are, not surprisingly, mixed in quality, but there are many encouraging signs that theological exegesis can produce readings that are nuanced in their attention to textual detail and simultaneously — *mirabile dictu* — nourishing for the church.

It is, however, not always clear exactly what is meant by the catchall term "theological exegesis." Someone might suggest that theological exegesis is like pornography: we don't know how to define it, but we know it when we see it. Perhaps it would be wise to leave it at that. But I think, on the contrary, that there may be value in offering some identifying characterization of the sort of exegesis that we are seeking to encourage and recover. There is a certain value in naming the goals we seek. In the remainder of this essay, then, I want to offer two things: (1) a brief description of the character of theological exegesis as I understand it, and (2) a couple of examples of my own recent attempts to read Scripture with eyes of faith.

III. What Is "Theological Exegesis"?

What makes exegesis "theological"? Theological exegesis is not a "method." It is not a set of discrete procedures that could be set alongside, say, textual criticism or redaction criticism. Rather, theological exegesis is a complex *practice,*[16] a way of approaching Scripture with eyes of faith and

---

useful entry points to the current discussion, see Davis and Hays, eds., *The Art of Reading Scripture;* Stephen E. Fowl, ed., *The Theological Interpretation of Scripture: Classic and Contemporary Readings* (Oxford: Blackwell, 1997); Brevard S. Childs, *The Struggle to Understand Isaiah as Christian Scripture* (Grand Rapids: Eerdmans, 2004); R. R. Reno, "Biblical Theology and Theological Exegesis," in *Out of Egypt: Biblical Theology and Biblical Interpretation,* ed. C. Bartholomew, M. Healy, K. Möller, and R. Parry (Scripture and Hermeneutics Series 5; Grand Rapids: Zondervan, 2004), pp. 385-408; Markus Bockmuehl, *Seeing the Word: Refocusing New Testament Study* (Grand Rapids: Baker Academic, 2006).

16. In the sense defined by Alasdair McIntyre: "By a practice I am going to mean any coherent and complex form of socially established co-operative human activity through which goods internal to that form of activity are realised in the course of trying to achieve those standards of excellence which are appropriate to, and partially definitive of, that form of activity, with the result that human powers to achieve excellence, and human conceptions

seeking to understand it within the community of faith. What are the salient identifying marks of this practice? For starters, I propose *twelve* such marks.

(1) Theological exegesis is *a practice of and for the church.* We lavish our attention on the biblical texts because these texts have been passed on to us by the church's tradition as the distinctive and irreplaceable testimony to events in which God has acted for our salvation. That is to say, theological exegesis regards these texts as *Scripture,* not merely as a collection of ancient writings whose content is of historical interest. A bare description of the ideational content of biblical writings ("the theology of Luke" or the like) is therefore not yet theological in the sense meant here. Theological exegesis, as Meeks rightly but disapprovingly notes, seeks to read the Bible as normative for a community.

(2) Theological exegesis is *self-involving discourse.* Interpreters who read the Bible theologically approach the text with an awareness that we are addressed and claimed by the word of God that is spoken in the text, and we understand ourselves to be answerable to that word. For that reason, exegesis that is authentically theological will frequently contain sentences that employ pronouns in the first and second persons. A strictly third-person form of discourse lends itself to the mode of pure description, in which the author may stand apart, uninvolved in the text's world. Theological exegesis, however, draws us into the world of the text and demands response. As self-involving confessional acts, theological readings are closely interwoven with the practice of *worship.*

(3) At the same time, *historical study is internal to the practice of theological exegesis.* The reasons why this is so are themselves fundamentally theological: God has created the material world, and God has acted for the redemption of that world through the incarnation of the Son in the historical person Jesus of Nazareth. History therefore cannot be either inimical or irrelevant to theology's affirmations of truth. The more accurately we understand the historical setting of first-century Palestine, the more precise and faithful will be our understanding of what the incarnate word

---

of the ends and goods involved, are systematically extended" (*After Virtue: A Study in Moral Theory,* 2nd ed. [Notre Dame: University of Notre Dame Press, 1984], p. 187).

taught, did, and suffered. The more we know about the Mediterranean world of Greco-Roman antiquity, the more nuanced will be our understanding of the ways in which the NT's epistles summoned their readers to a conversion of the imagintion.[17]

(4) Theological exegesis attends to *the literary wholeness of the individual scriptural witnesses.* This, I would propose to you, is one of the signature contributions of biblical studies over the past fifty years to the task of theology. The Bible must be read neither as an anthology of disconnected theological sound-bites nor, on the other hand, as a single undifferentiated story. Nor can its message be adequately grasped only through excerpts encountered in the church's liturgy. Rather, the Bible contains a chorus of different voices, and the distinctive integrity of each part in the chorus is essential to its polyphonic performance. This is especially true for texts such as the Gospels, which come to us in the form of cohesive narratives. It matters, as Irenaeus insisted, that we have not a single homogenized Gospel but rather a fourfold Gospel, in which the discrete voices of Matthew, Mark, Luke, and John can and must be heard. Theological exegesis attends lovingly to the distinctive testimony of each witness.

(5) My fifth point is the dialectical converse of the previous one: Theological exegesis can never be content only to describe the theological perspectives of the individual biblical authors; instead, it always presses forward to *the synthetic question of canonical coherence.* This does not mean, of course, the assimilation of everything to a single doctrinal norm, as has happened sometimes when, for example, justification *sola fide* is made the single lens for interpreting all biblical texts. But it does mean that the theological exegete will seek the big picture, asking how any particular text fits into the larger biblical story of God's gracious action. (This is one of the points at which Luke Timothy Johnson and I have consistently differed: he believes we can simply listen to each canonical witness separately and then move directly to contemporary appropriation, whereas I would insist that Christian theological exegesis has historically sought to allow

17. See R. B. Hays, *The Conversion of the Imagination: Paul as Interpreter of Israel's Scripture* (Grand Rapids: Eerdmans, 2005).

the different biblical witnesses to "talk to each other" and to articulate some sort of complex unity.)[18]

(6) Theological exegesis does not focus chiefly on the hypothetical history behind the biblical texts, nor does it attend primarily to the meaning of texts as self-contained works of literature; rather, it focuses on these *texts as testimony.* That means we need to learn to stand where these witnesses stand and look where they point. Insofar as we do this, we will learn to see *as* they see; as Minear's *Eyes of Faith* promises, we will find our vision trained anew. If we read the texts as testimony, we will find ourselves constantly reminded that the Bible is chiefly about God, not about human religious aspirations and power struggles.[19]

(7) *The language of theological exegesis is intratextual in character.*[20] In intratextual theological exegesis, our interpretations will remain close to the primary language of the witnesses, rather than moving away from the particularity of the biblical testimony to a language of second-order abstraction that seeks to "translate" the biblical imagery into some other conceptual register. Of course, this sort of "translation" project was at the heart of Bultmann's hermeneutical program; however laudable its intention, it was theologically vacuous and unfruitful. One of R. R. Reno's chief complaints about many contemporary failed attempts at theological exegesis is that they commit precisely this same "translation" fallacy, without the same hermeneutical sophistication displayed in Bultmann's work.[21]

18. See, e.g., Luke Timothy Johnson and William S. Kurz, S.J., *The Future of Catholic Biblical Scholarship: A Constructive Conversation* (Grand Rapids: Eerdmans, 2002), pp. 129-30; cf. R. B. Hays, *The Moral Vision of the New Testament* (San Francisco: HarperSanFrancisco, 1996), pp. 187-205.

19. See the first thesis of the Scripture Project, which declares that "God is the primary agent revealed in the biblical narrative" (Davis and Hays, *Art of Reading Scripture,* p. 1).

20. I use the term "intratextual" in the sense explained by George Lindbeck, *The Nature of Doctrine: Religion and Theology in a Postliberal Age* (Philadelphia: Westminster, 1984): "Intratextual theology describes reality within the Scriptural framework, rather than translating Scripture into extrascriptural categories. It is the text, so to speak, which absorbs the world, rather than the world the text" (p. 118).

21. Reno, "Biblical Theology" (see n. 15, above), *passim.* His essay gives dozens of examples, of which I cite only one for purposes of illustration: whereas Paul in Romans 8:26-27 declares that the Spirit helps us in our weakness and intercedes with God, Luke Johnson's com-

(8) Theological exegesis, insofar it stays close to the language and conceptuality of the NT witnesses, will find itself drawn into the Bible's complex web of *intertextuality*. The NT insistently cites and alludes to the OT, argues for a narrative continuity between the story of Israel and the story of Jesus, and interprets that continuity through discerning *typological* correspondences between the two. Consequently, theological exegesis will have to concern itself with tracing and interpreting these complex intertextual correspondences between the testaments.

(9) Theological exegesis thereby is committed to the discovery and exposition of *multiple senses* in biblical texts. Old Testament texts, when read in conjunction with the story of Jesus, take on new and unexpected resonances as they prefigure events far beyond the historical horizon of their authors and original readers. The NT's stories of Jesus, when understood as mysterious fulfillments of long-ago promises, assume a depth beyond their literal sense as reports of events of the recent past. Texts have multiple layers of meaning that are disclosed by the Holy Spirit to faithful and patient readers.[22]

(10) Learning to read the text with eyes of faith is a skill for which we are trained by *the Christian tradition*. Consequently, theological exegesis knows itself to be part of an ancient and lively conversation. We can never approach the Bible as though we are the first ones to read it — or the first to read it appropriately. We know that we have much to learn from the wisdom of those who have reflected deeply on these texts before us. Consequently, *theological exegesis will find hermeneutical aid, not hindrance, in the church's doctrinal traditions.*[23]

---

mentary on the passage transposes the categories into a discussion of "intimacy between the divine and human freedom" (L. T. Johnson, *Reading Romans: A Literary and Theological Commentary* [Reading the New Testament; New York: Crossroad, 1997], p. 131, cited in Reno, p. 391). This sort of move to the language of secondary reflectivity is not in itself inappropriate; indeed, it may be in some ways necessary. The difficulty appears when such language overshadows or supplants the primary language of the text on which it is intended to comment.

22. Cf. the fourth thesis of the Scripture Project: "Texts of Scripture do not have a single meaning limited to the intent of the original author. In accord with Jewish and Christian traditions, we affirm that Scripture has multiple complex senses given by God, the author of the whole drama" (Davis and Hays, *Art of Reading Scripture*, p. 2).

23. For a defense of this claim, see D. S. Yeago, "The New Testament and the Nicene

(11) Theological exegesis, however, goes beyond repeating traditional interpretations; rather, instructed by the example of traditional readings, theological interpreters will produce *fresh readings,* new performances of Scripture's sense; they will encounter the texts anew with eyes of faith and see the ways that the Holy Spirit continues to speak to the churches through the same ancient texts that the tradition has handed on to us. To put the same point in a slightly different way, the Spirit-led imagination, an imagination converted by the word, is an essential faculty for the work of theological exegesis.

(12) Finally, when we speak of theological exegesis, particularly when we acknowledge the Spirit's role, we must always remember that we are speaking not chiefly of our own clever readings and constructions of the text, but rather of the way that God, working through the text, is re-shaping us. In his foreword to a recent collection of Minear's essays, J. Louis Martyn quotes the famous dictum of Johann Albrecht Bengel, "Apply yourself wholly to the text; apply the text wholly to yourself." Martyn, however, proposes that the maxim should be reworded to read, "Apply yourself wholly to the text, and the text will apply itself wholly to you!"[24] If it is true, as we confess with the author of the Letter to the Hebrews, that "the word of God is living and active, sharper than any two-edged sword" (Heb. 4:12), then we may indeed expect to be transformed as we read. This means that theological exegesis must always be done from a posture of prayer and humility before the word. In the preface to the English edition of his Romans commentary, Karl Barth asks whom or what his book should serve. Here is how he answers the question: "No doubt it should be of service to those who read it. But, primarily and above all else, it must serve that *other* Book where Jesus Christ is present in His Church. Theology is *ministerium verbi divini.* It is nothing more

---

Dogma: A Contribution to the Recovery of Theological Exegesis," in *The Theological Interpretation of Scripture: Classic and Contemporary Readings,* ed. S. E. Fowl (Oxford: Blackwell, 1997). Fowl's edited collection is itself testimony to the point I am making here. For a recent and particularly illuminating case study, see B. S. Childs, *The Struggle to Understand Isaiah as Christian Scripture.*

24. J. L. Martyn, "Foreword" to P. S. Minear, *The Bible and the Historian: Breaking the Silence About God in Biblical Studies* (Nashville: Abingdon, 2002), p. 11.

nor less."[25] If that is true of theology in general, surely it is true *a fortiori* for theological exegesis.

IV. "Go and Tell What You Have Seen and Heard": Theological Exegesis in Practice

In the final part of this essay, I want to attempt an actual act of reading that will seek to illustrate theological exegesis in practice. I shall not at every point explain how this reading exemplifies the identifying marks of theological exegesis that I have just described, but I hope that some of the connections will be evident.

It has become a conventional view in modern NT criticism that the Gospel of Luke represents a "low" or "primitive" christology.[26] According to this view, Luke portrays Jesus as a Spirit-anointed prophet, a teacher of divine wisdom, and a righteous martyr. Lacking, however, are any doctrines of preexistence and incarnation; lacking is any clear assertion of Jesus' identity with God. As we shall see, an attentive theological exegesis of Luke's Gospel gives us substantial reason to question this characterization of Lukan christology.

In Luke 7:18-23, the imprisoned John the Baptist sends messengers to question Jesus about his identity.[27] They ask, as John has instructed them,

---

25. K. Barth, *The Epistle to the Romans* (London: Oxford, 1933), p. x.

26. For a representative view, see, e.g., John Drury, "Luke, Gospel of," in *A Dictionary of Biblical Interpretation*, ed. R. J. Coggins and J. L. Houlden (London: SCM, 1990), pp. 410-13. Drury writes, "It has long been noticed that [Luke] has a 'lower' christology than the other evangelists, and a much lower one than John." Similarly, Christopher M. Tuckett observes, "Many have argued that, insofar as Luke's views can be discerned, the picture is fundamentally a 'subordinationist' one: Jesus is presented as above all a human being who is subordinate to God" ("The Christology of Luke-Acts," in *The Unity of Luke-Acts*, ed. Joseph Verheyden [Leuven: Leuven University Press, 1999], pp. 133-64 [quotation from pp. 148-49]).

27. A nearly identical account appears in Matthew 11:2-6. This passage therefore belongs to material sometimes designated as coming from the hypothetical Q source. I am one of those who have serious doubts about the Q hypothesis, and in any case our chief concern here is not with source-critical issues. Unfortunately, time does not permit a comparison of the slightly different ways this story functions within Luke and Matthew; instead, our particular focus will be on theological exegesis of the passage in its *Lukan* setting.

"Are you ὁ ἐρχόμενος, 'the Coming One,' or shall we look for another?" The question is given particular emphasis by its repetition in verses 19 and 20 (in contrast to Matt. 11:3); this is a good example of Luke's emulation of OT narrative style, but it also serves the important purpose of forcing the reader to linger over the question and to ponder its significance, particularly the significance of the term ὁ ἐρχόμενος. The carefully chosen language of the question evokes Psalm 118:26 (= Ps. 117:26 LXX), which is the culminating doxological passage of the cycle of Hallel Psalms (Ps. 113–18): "Blessed is ὁ ἐρχόμενος in the name of the Lord." The Hallel Psalms were sung on the occasion of Israel's great national festivals of Tabernacles and Passover. Both of these festivals were associated with Israel's national liberation from bondage in Egypt and therefore also — in the first-century context — linked with the hope of a future liberation from Roman rule and the coming of a new king. Luke, more clearly than the other Synoptic Gospels, makes this royal hope fully explicit in his account of Jesus' triumphal entry to Jerusalem, as the crowd chants, using the words of Psalm 118:26, "Blessed is ὁ ἐρχόμενος, *the king* who comes in the name of the Lord" (Luke 19:38).[28] Thus, reading retrospectively in the context of Luke's narrative, we see that John the Baptist's question in Luke 7:19-20 is a politically loaded query: he is asking whether Jesus intends to proclaim himself Israel's long-awaited ruler who will restore the kingdom of David. John is asking, "Are you the Coming One, the coming King?"

Jesus' answer speaks volumes without answering the question directly: "Go and tell John what you have seen and heard: the blind receive their sight, the lame walk, the lepers are cleansed, the deaf hear, the dead are raised, the poor have good news brought to them. And blessed is anyone who takes no offense at me" (Luke 7:23). The answer makes sense only when we recognize that it echoes a number of motifs drawn from *Isaiah's* portrayal of the end of Israel's exile and God's eschatological restoration of the nation. The first and most important echo should remind John's emissaries of Isaiah 35:5-6a:

---

28. Only Luke here has ὁ βασιλεύς as an explanatory gloss on "the Coming One" (cf. Matt. 21:9, Mark 11:10).

Then the eyes of the blind shall be opened,
and the ears of the deaf unstopped;
then the lame shall leap like a deer,
and the tongue of the speechless sing for joy.

These stirring images are part of Isaiah's vision of the exiled Israelites returning on a miraculous highway through the desert to Zion. Isaiah paints
a picture of God's healing all that is broken, putting all things right in the
eschatological time. The great Charles Wesley hymn "O for a Thousand
Tongues" draws on precisely these images:

Hear him ye deaf, his praise, ye dumb,
your loosened tongues employ;
Ye blind, behold your Savior come,
and leap, ye lame, for joy.[29]

But Jesus' answer also sounds a second, slightly less prominent echo in the
phrase "the poor have good news proclaimed to them." The Greek expression here, πτωχοὶ εὐαγγελίζονται, reminds us of the passage from Isaiah 61
that Jesus had earlier read in the synagogue in Nazareth to inaugurate his
public ministry:

The Spirit of the Lord is upon me,
because he has anointed me to proclaim good news to the poor
(εὐαγγελίσασθαι πτωχοῖς);
he has sent me to proclaim release to the captives,
and recovery of sight to the blind.[30]

On that occasion, Jesus had stunningly announced, "Today, this Scripture
has been fulfilled in your hearing" (Luke 4:16-21). Thus, in Luke 7, Jesus' ap-

29. Charles Wesley, *The United Methodist Hymnal* (Nashville: United Methodist Publishing House, 1989), 57.

30. The text of Isaiah 61 cited in Luke 4:18-19 follows the LXX much more closely than
the MT, and it also includes a fragmentary echo of Isaiah 58:6 ("to let the oppressed go
free"), as well as an allusion to the year of Jubilee (Lev. 25:10). Each of these observations is
of interest for the interpretation of Luke 4, but the scope of the present essay precludes pur-
suing them in further detail.

parently cryptic response to John's disciples is actually a very clear, intertextually coded response.[31] By evoking Isaiah 35 and Isaiah 61, Jesus offers a scriptural interpretive framework for the miraculous deeds that John's disciples have seen him perform. The passages from Isaiah should signal to John — or to any hearer steeped in Israel's scriptures — that Jesus' activity is indeed to be understood as the inauguration of the coming kingdom of God for which Israel had longed and for which John was waiting.

Yet these passages at the very same time gesture towards a dramatic reshaping of Israel's national hope. The motifs selected by Jesus in his answer to John's disciples pointedly avoid images of military conquest. They focus instead on actions of healing and restoration.[32] Precisely by doing so, they offer John and his followers a new, nonviolent image of "the Coming One" and teach them to read Israel's Scripture with new eyes. In effect, Jesus' act of teaching John's messengers how to "read" his own ministry in light of Isaiah's words is *in itself* part of his work of opening the eyes of the blind.

The concluding macarism, "blessed is he who takes no offense at me" (μὴ σκανδαλισθῇ ἐν ἐμοί, literally "is not caused to stumble in me") should probably be understood as yet another echo — this time, pointing to Isaiah's image of the stone laid in Zion (Isa. 28:16), which will also be a stone of stumbling for Israel (Isa. 8:14; cf. the fusion of these two texts in Rom. 9:32-33). Isaiah's famous and enigmatic "stone" image draws a sharp contrast between the prophet's trust in God's promise and Israel's faithless reliance on military power as a source of security. The point is that John and his disciples should not "stumble" over Jesus' unexpected peaceful way of bringing in God's promised reign. (Luke later underscores his point narratively by telling the story of the two disciples on the road to Emmaus, who are leaving Jerusalem in disappointment *despite* having heard the report of the empty tomb. They say, "we had hoped that he was the one to redeem Israel" [Luke 24:21a]; that is, they had been expecting the conventional

---

31. For a full listing of the allusive parallels, see Dale C. Allison, Jr., *The Intertextual Jesus: Scripture in Q* (Harrisburg, PA: Trinity Press International, 2000), pp. 109-14.

32. The Dead Sea Scrolls have now yielded up evidence that other Jewish interpreters of this era drew upon precisely these same Isaianic texts as a description of the Lord's saving actions in the eschatological age. See particularly 4Q521.

royal military redeemer.) The writer of the nineteenth-century hymn "Lead on, O King Eternal" gets the point just right:

> For not with swords loud clashing, nor roll of stirring drums;
> with deeds of love and mercy the heavenly kingdom comes.[33]

Luke sketches all this with economy of language and literary power through allusion and metalepsis.[34] The reader who knows the Psalter and Isaiah will get the point well enough. In light of the echoes from Psalm 118 and Isaiah, the answer that we as readers are to supply to John's question is something like this: "Is Jesus the Coming One? Yes, he is the Coming King to which Psalm 118 points, the eschatological deliverer anticipated every time the Hallel Psalms are sung. He is the one for whom we have hoped, but his coming Kingdom must be interpreted not in terms of violent or coercive power, but in light of Isaiah's images of divine mercy and restoration."

There remains one more important thing to be said about this text. Jesus' answer to John hints at one more, still deeper truth at the heart of the good news Jesus is proclaiming. The texts from the prophet Isaiah that echo in Jesus' answer also adumbrate *the return of the LORD to Zion.* Israel is to be saved, according to Isaiah, not by a merely human leader who will bring them back from exile; rather, *God himself* will appear on the scene to lead the triumphant procession of returning exiles. As we have already seen, Jesus alludes forcefully to Isaiah 35:5 ("then the eyes of the blind shall be opened, and the ears of the deaf unstopped"). But *how* will these saving acts occur? Listen to the verse just before this, Isaiah 35:4: "Say to those who are of a fearful heart, 'Be strong, do not fear! *Here is your God. . . . He will come and save you.*'" Should we hear this echo as a metaleptic hint that the identity of this Coming One is something far greater than what John the Baptist envisioned?

---

33. E. W. Shurtleff, "Lead On, O King Eternal," *The United Methodist Hymnal,* 580.

34. *Metalepsis* is a literary device in which an author quotes only a part of a precursor text, in such a way that the reader or hearer must recall the larger context from which the citation comes in order to grasp its full import. For further discussion, see R. B. Hays, *Echoes of Scripture in the Letters of Paul* (New Haven: Yale University Press, 1989), pp. 14-21; idem, *The Conversion of the Imagination: Paul as Interpreter of Israel's Scripture* (Grand Rapids: Eerdmans, 2005), pp. 2-3, and esp. n. 5.

The suggestion may seem far-fetched until we consider more broadly the way in which the Evangelist Luke subtly narrates the identity of Jesus throughout his Gospel. Luke is the only one of the Gospel writers who regularly uses κύριος as a title for Jesus. Κύριος is, of course, the Greek word used by the Septuagint to translate the holy name of God, the Tetragrammaton (often dubiously rendered in modern English translations as "Yahweh"). There are at least fifteen instances in Luke where the Evangelist refers to Jesus as the κύριος.[35] Consider the following examples: "And why has this happened to me, that the mother of *my Lord* comes to me?" (Luke 1:43); ". . . to you is born this day in the city of David a Savior, who is Christ *the Lord*" (2:11); "when *the Lord* saw her, he had compassion on her" (7:13); "Mary sat at *the Lord*'s feet" (10:39); "*The Lord* turned and looked at Peter" (22:61); "*The Lord* has risen indeed" (24:34). Most appositely, within the very passage we are considering, we find this: "John summoned two of his disciples, and sent them to *the Lord* to ask . . ." (7:18b-19a). In short, Luke quite remarkably applies the title κύριος both to the God of Israel[36] and to Jesus of Nazareth — occasionally in a way that suggests a mysterious fusion of divine and human identity in the figure of Jesus.[37]

The hermeneutical effect of Luke's repeated narrative usage of κύριος is not unlike the effect achieved at the end of Paul's Christ-hymn in Philippians 2, which astonishingly ascribes to Jesus the eschatological Lordship that Isaiah 45:23 emphatically reserves for God alone: "so that at the name of Jesus every knee should bend . . . and every tongue should confess that Jesus Christ is *Kyrios*, to the glory of God the Father" (Phil. 2:10-11). In that same confession, Luke invites us to join. Consequently, when Jesus says to John's messengers "Blessed is the one who takes no offense in me" (Luke 7:23), his blessing answers in call-and-response fashion

---

35. This tally does not count the vocative κύριε and other ambiguous instances.

36. Examples are numerous. Especially clear is Luke 1:16: "He will turn many of the people of Israel to *the Lord* their God."

37. For a thorough, theologically sophisticated analysis of this striking phenomenon in Lukan narrative christology, see C. Kavin Rowe, *Early Narrative Christology: The Lord in the Gospel of Luke* (BZNW 139; Berlin: De Gruyter, 2006). For an earlier concise preview of his observations, see idem, "Luke and the Trinity: An Essay in Ecclesial Biblical Theology," *SJT* 56 (2003): 1-26.

the very text to which John's question alluded, Psalm 118:26: "Blessed is the Coming One, the One who comes in the name of the *Kyrios.*" It turns out, beyond all possible human power of anticipation, that Jesus is *both* ὁ ἐρχόμενος, the Coming One *and*, in embodied form, ὁ κύριος, the LORD.

In view of these exegetical findings, I would hazard the following conclusion: the "low" christology that modernist criticism has perceived in Luke's Gospel is an artificial construction achieved by excluding the hermeneutical relevance of the wider canonical witness, particularly the OT allusions in Luke's story. It is precisely by attending more fully to the *Old Testament* allusions in Luke's Gospel that we gain a deeper and firmer grasp of the theological coherence between Luke's testimony and what the church's dogmatic tradition has affirmed about the identity of Jesus.

And so, though we may be imprisoned and beset by doubt, though the time of the kingdom's coming seems slow, though the power of violence still seems to rule, we are taught by Luke — when his Gospel is read within the intertextual network to which it points — to recognize Jesus, the one who brings good news to the poor, as our LORD. And recognizing that, we find our eyes, like the eyes of the disciples on the road to Emmaus, opened to see in Moses and all the prophets the truth of the Gospel's testimony: "Be strong, do not fear! *Here is your God. . . . He will come and save you.*"

Contributors

Thomas Breidenthal is the Bishop of the Diocese of Southern Ohio, Episcopal Church USA. He was formerly Dean of Religious Life and of the Chapel at Princeton University. He has been an active participant in Jewish-Christian-Muslim dialogue for many years, and is also the author of *Christian Households: The Sanctification of Nearness* (Cowley, 1997/Wipf and Stock, 2004) and *Sacred Unions: A New Guide to Lifelong Commitment* (Cowley Publications, 2006).

James J. Buckley is Professor of Theology and Dean of the College of Arts and Sciences at Loyola College in Maryland. He has recently contributed to and edited (with Frederick Bauerschmidt and Trent Pomplun) *The Blackwell Companion to Catholicism* (Blackwell, 2007). He is associate director of the Center for Catholic and Evangelical Theology.

Ellen F. Davis is Professor of Bible and Practical Theology at Duke Divinity School. A lay Episcopalian, she teaches and preaches on topics relating to the church's use of Scripture. Her most recent book is *Scripture, Culture, and Agriculture: An Agrarian Reading of the Bible* (Cambridge, 2008).

Richard B. Hays is the George Washington Ivey Professor of New Testament, The Divinity School, Duke University.

Robert Jenson was Senior Scholar for Research at the Center of Theological Inquiry (Princeton, N.J.) from 1998 to 2005 and previously taught at St.

Olaf College (1988-1998) and Lutheran Theological Seminary in Gettysburg, PA (1968-1988). Among his publications are a two-volume *Systematic Theology* (Oxford University Press, 1997-1999) and more recently *Conversation with Poppi,* with his eight-year-old granddaughter Solveig Lucia Gold (Brazos Press, 2006).

Amy Plantinga Pauw is Henry P. Mobley, Jr., Professor of Doctrinal Theology at Louisville Presbyterian Seminary and a member of the Presbyterian Church U.S.A. She recently edited *Feminist and Womanist Essays in Reformed Dogmatics* with Serene Jones and has also published on Jonathan Edwards and Christian practices. She will serve as a consulting editor for Westminster John Knox Press's new theological commentary on the Bible series, for which she will write the volume on Proverbs and Ecclesiastes.

R. R. Reno is Professor of Theological Ethics at Creighton University, Omaha, NE. With John O'Keefe he is the author of *Sanctified Vision: An Introduction to Early Christian Interpretation of the Bible* (Johns Hopkins University Press, 2005).

Michael Root is Dean and Vice-President for Academic Affairs at Lutheran Theological Southern Seminary, Columbia, SC. He is Executive Director of the Center for Catholic and Evangelical Theology.